SURVIVE THE UNTHINKABLE

SURVIVE THE UNTHINKABLE

A Total Guide to Women's Self-Protection

Tim Larkin

Foreword by Tony Robbins

RODALE.

Rodale books may be purchased for business or promotional use or for special sales.
For information, please write to:
Special Markets Department, Rodale Inc., 733 Third Avenue, New York, NY 10017.

Printed in the United States of America
Rodale Inc. makes every effort to use acid-free ♾, recycled paper ♻.

Book design by Christina L. Gaugler
Illustration by Karen Kuchar

Library of Congress Cataloging-in-Publication Data is on file with the publisher.
ISBN-13: 978–1–60961–358–7 paperback

Distributed to the trade by Macmillan
2   4   6   8   10   9   7   5   3   1   paperback

We inspire and enable people to improve their lives and the world around them.
rodalebooks.com

To the memory of Joie Ruth Armstrong, 26, naturalist with the Yosemite Institute, who was murdered in July 1999.

When confronted, she fought for her life against a bigger, stronger man with a weapon. Even when subdued, bound, and gagged, she managed to escape from a moving car and made it 150 yards into the woods before being overrun.

Her story affects me deeply because she had the athletic ability, the will to survive, and the motivation to do the work—she absolutely expended more than enough effort to destroy him—she just didn't know where to focus that effort.

She died not from weakness or cowardice but from a lack of useful information.

All too often we remember the predators but not their victims. Joie is more important than her killer because her life prior to this event and the valiant effort she exhibited in her actions at the end of it serve as models and motivators for the rest of us—motivation to train, motivation to learn how to make a difference, motivation to act.

My intent with this book is to provide you with that useful information Joie lacked.

Contents

FOREWORD

Violence against women remains one of the most common human rights abuses in the world. Women ages 15 through 44 are more likely to die or be maimed because of male violence than because of cancer, malaria, war, and traffic accidents combined.

Rape and attempted rape are very much silent assassins. Only 16 percent of rape victims actually report an incident to the police, which means that the statistics we have about rape in the United States barely reflect the grim reality. The World Health Organization has found that domestic and sexual violence affects 30 to 60 percent of women in most countries. And the majority of offenses are committed by someone the victim knows or at least recognizes.

Perhaps the most disturbing truth is that the rape perpetrator will probably victimize seven to nine women before he's jailed.

In our increasingly violent collective, women must often yield to an incessant voice that warns: *Be careful where you walk. Be careful where you park. Be careful where you go. Be careful what you wear. Be careful what you say. . .*

The unnerving posture of gender violence is what prompted me to seek out the best self-defense instructor I could find for the women I care about in my life—who just happens to be the author of the book you're holding in your hands right now.

Tim Larkin's *Survive the Unthinkable* relays a message of empowerment, not panic. It's the key that can unlock your personal power as a woman.

With many things in life, the truth is often nearly 180 degrees from what your imagination might suggest. The principles and methods that Tim Larkin shares in this critical book are perfect examples of this:

⟡ Women need NOT be vulnerable to attack, and they *already* have the tools necessary to avoid violence or protect themselves in those rare instances where avoidance isn't possible.

⟡ Even the most violent sociopaths are incredibly vulnerable once you know the psychology of what drives their behavior.

⟡ The people who are most effective at "self-defense" typically have no formal training.

Being able to protect yourself doesn't require muscle, fancy techniques, or months of practice at the martial arts studio. All that you need to live confidently and joyfully is knowledge and the willingness to apply it.

As a woman, you have people who depend on you—perhaps your partner, children, siblings, friends—please consider the ability to defend yourself a *responsibility*, not a luxury, in much the same way that you might exercise, wear your seatbelt, or get regular medical checkups.

This book presents imperative components that ensure peace of mind, which ultimately allows us to find fulfillment in our daily life. The emotional edge my friend Tim Larkin presents helps to create a better life through key adjustments to our perception, psychology, and awareness. You can trust, as I do, that Tim Larkin's teachings are the most effective, thoroughly tested, and reliable way to ensure your safety, confidence, and self-assurance, which will in turn enable you to effectively cooperate with others, operate at optimal productivity, and get the most enjoyment out of every day of your life.

May you walk through life without fear and live with passion!

Tony Robbins
The world's #1 peak performance coach and life strategist

INTRODUCTION

I dedicated this book to Joie Ruth Armstrong, the woman who was murdered by a serial killer in Yosemite National Park. Her story is worth remembering as a cautionary tale. But the real reason I wrote this book was for you—for every woman who wants to live a long and happy life, safe from any danger. My message to you is this: You can successfully defeat a bigger, stronger assailant. Knowing *how* to injure him is the key.

The advice "Fighting back will make him mad" is outdated and has been disproven in the most recent study (commissioned in 2005) issued by the National Institute of Justice. It found that fighting back does not necessarily mean a woman is more likely to be injured; it is, in fact, the best way to survive a violent attack. This same report estimated that 1.9 million women are physically assaulted in the United States annually, yet self-defense books still advocate cooperating or screaming—not attacking.

Survive the Unthinkable bridges this gap by offering a field-tested system of training that enables you to go on the offense during a life-threatening encounter and greatly improves your chances of walking away from it. It shows you how to *protect* yourself—so you won't end up a victim of violence.

If you travel alone, work late hours, or simply live in our modern world, you must face this sobering fact: According to a press release from the White House (declaring April 2009 National Sexual Assault Awareness Month), 18 percent of women in this country have been raped. According to the Rape, Abuse & Incest National Network (RAINN), the nation's largest anti–sexual violence organization, one out of every six American women has been the victim of an attempted or completed rape; this translates to 17.7 million American women. Every two minutes, someone in the United States is sexually assaulted, and more than 50 percent of all rapes/sexual assaults occur within one mile of or at the victim's home. Now, that's scary stuff.

The National Institute of Justice has stated that certain techniques reduce the risk of rape more than 80 percent. Ironically, these "certain techniques" (which require causing injury) are generally found in testosterone-soaked books that aren't intended for women. *Survive the Unthinkable* rectifies this by presenting this critical knowledge directly to you—as a woman, you're a full-fledged member of the most underserved group in the self-defense category.

Chances are, everything you've been told about self-defense is a lie. You have probably been told that you are the weaker sex and that your options are to defend yourself by screaming to attract attention, running away, talking him down, or pretending you have a male companion just out of sight. You may have also been told not to counter a predator, to do what he says, to hand over your wallet, and not to rock the boat.

Not only are these methods completely absurd, but they may get you killed! While 1.9 million women are physically assaulted in the United States annually, most women are unprepared for a violent encounter.

You may be familiar with some of the following common responses to the concept of being attacked or may even have thought them yourself:

⋄ If I am ever attacked, I will just try to reason with them and give them what they want—surely they will go away.

⋄ If I am attacked, I will scream at the top of my lungs and just try to avoid getting in the car.

⋄ If I am attacked, I will pretend that my boyfriend is on the phone with me. I always carry my cell phone in my hand for that very purpose.

⋄ I won't be attacked—I carry Mace in my purse.

⋄ I have no idea what I would do if I was attacked.

The problem with all these thoughts is that they are all absolutely ineffective, and they leave you with no real plan. During a truly violent encounter, you have *only seconds to act*, and the things mentioned above won't save your life against a predator. What *will* save your life is changing the way you perceive violence, and learning how to actually think like a predator, in order to avoid one or, if necessary, protect yourself from one.

Generally speaking, violence is stigmatized in law-abiding society. That's a good thing! But it also means that the only people who know how to use the tool most effectively are predators. And, unlike most people, predators don't play by the rules of society. They are willing to take everything you have—including your life.

I wrote this book thinking about every woman who, no matter how smart and tough, has found herself in a vulnerable position doing everyday activities. We have all had a situation where the hairs on the back of our head stood on end and we clutched our keys as a weapon or gripped our cell phone just a little harder. Maybe it was when the elevator closed and you found yourself alone with a creepy guy, or while you had your back turned at the ATM, or when a blind date lingered a little too long at the front door. After safely locking your door, you asked yourself, "What would I have done if he'd pushed his way in?"

Survive the Unthinkable gives you concrete knowledge on how to avoid dangerous situations and concrete plans for how to act, should you encounter them. Learning to injure an attacker won't make you violent. It's a tool that will help you walk taller and live safely. You don't buy a fire extinguisher because you want to fight fires—you buy one because you want to be prepared in case a fire occurs.

Every woman can be her own best insurance policy, and understanding the information in this book changes your perception of what violence is, how it works—and what *you* can do to prevent it from happening to you.

I am a close-combat expert, and I travel extensively across the country and around the world to teach my system of self-protection: Target Focus Training (TFT). All kinds of people train with me: Navy SEALs, CEOs, even kindergarten teachers.

I want to make sure that if you're ever in a violent situation, you can walk away with your life. Now, I'm talking about real violence, the situations we pretend won't happen to us, the things we don't like to talk about—but as I've stated above, they do happen, and you should be prepared in case the unthinkable ever does happen.

Although women are most often the targets of violence, in my teaching I have found that very few have any practical training on how to deal with it. They want to learn how to defend themselves, but typical self-defense classes emphasize *reacting* to an attacker: "Talk your way out of danger," or "Don't get him mad," or "Pretend your husband is just moments away." These ideas may get you out of a nonlethal jam (and I'll cover the difference between lethal violence and nonlethal violence in more detail in Chapter Two). But I know from experience that when a threat *is* lethal, these self-defense skills are worthless.

I don't teach self-defense. I focus solely on what you must do to save yourself when social skills won't work—a life-threatening situation. I teach my clients to *defeat* the threat, to stop violence from happening to them.

In this book, you are going to learn a comprehensive training methodology designed with one goal in mind: to give you the ability to survive a life-or-death situation. It doesn't take years to learn, require special athletic skills, or demand daily practice. It isn't based on "cool" techniques seen in movies or on fighting styles suited for martial arts competitions—it relies on what works in a given situation, and there are no rules except enabling your own survival. This effective approach to self-protection is counterintuitive for many women: I teach you to move closer to an attacker, injure him, and take control of a violent situation.

Put simply: This is a method of selecting targets on the human body and striking them to injure and elicit a universal spinal reflex response. You don't need to be big and strong—in fact, your size doesn't matter at all. Have you ever been head-butted by a baby? It hurts! An instructor of mine—all 270 pounds of him—nearly dropped his year-old daughter after she clocked him, his reaction was so severe.

If a small child can do damage, imagine the hurt that can be accomplished by a grown woman trained to hit specific body targets! A five-foot woman can absolutely take down a six-foot man . . . if she knows where to strike him. There are more than seventy different anatomical areas on the human body that, if injured, create a spinal reflex that incapacitates someone, regardless of size or strength. I'll cover this in more detail, too.

I teach this controversial—yet devastatingly effective—approach because violence exists, as much as we'd like to believe otherwise. It happens quickly, and you have about five seconds to react. You can use those moments to think, "I can't believe this is happening to me!" or you can take immediate, life-saving action while simultaneously thinking, "I am going to make *this* [an attack-stopping injury] happen to *him*!"

This approach to self-protection trains you to go on "automatic," so you hurt your attacker first—*before* you get seriously injured or killed. This may sound too good to be true, but I assure you that it is 100 percent possible. I train women of every shape and size, both athletes and couch potatoes. All of them can successfully protect themselves from a physical assault against an attacker of any size. Gaining this ability removes a subconscious burden for women: You no longer live in fear of the unknown, of becoming a horrible statistic. If the worst happens, you know what to do to save your own life.

As a final note, I'd like to emphasize that the goal of this training method is not to go out looking for trouble; waiting, taut with menace, for that guy's eye to twitch wrong so you can pounce on him. I doubt this is your intent—but I want to reiterate that causing injury should be used only as a last resort— when your life is threatened. The most compelling reason to learn how to injure another human being is one I have heard many times from the women who have completed my training courses: It gives you ultimate control over your own life.

Ready? Let's get started.

SURVIVE THE UNTHINKABLE

CHAPTER ONE

WHEN THE UNTHINKABLE HAPPENS

L ife, in many ways, is like a game. We all live by a set of rules that govern sane, socialized behavior, and when we all play by these rules, people live happy lives in relative safety. These rules are, in essence, a set of agreements that we have with each other. For example, on the road we all agree to stop at red lights and drive on the right side of the painted line. When we fail to abide by these rules, people often get hurt or killed.

Most of us live according to age-old agreements about ethical behavior—think of the Ten Commandments or the Golden Rule. All societies have remarkably similar ethical codes when it comes to civilized behavior. From a very early age, we are taught these rules until they become part of our social DNA.

The problem with this whole agreement scenario is that obviously, not everyone plays along. There are those among us who do not recognize or abide by the rules the rest of us acknowledge and respect. These individuals are predators. In some cases, predators have consciences, and in other cases, they do not. Asocial predators know how to capitalize on your desire to be a decent, ethical person so they can use it against you to get what they want.

THE FEMALE ADVANTAGE

As a woman, you have a special gift—an advantage, really—that many men do not. Most women, even at a very early age, are remarkably good at reading and interpreting the significance of nonverbal cues: body language, posture, gait, expression, grooming, clothing choices, and so on. By comparison, most men are almost comically inept when it comes to reading all but the most overt signals. Whereas men's ability to read nonverbal cues is essentially like a binary code—they either see it or they don't—women are able to pick up on a rainbow of nuanced signals, as if they're seeing everything in full color while men are seeing in black-and-white.

Think of this set of typically female skills as a natural early warning mechanism (I often describe it as radar) that gives you precious moments to *avoid* violence instead of needing to deal with it on a physical level. My goal in this book is to make you aware of the many different types of potentially violent behavior.

Asocial violence is designed to be difficult to spot—which is why you need to trust and use your radar so you'll never end up in a dangerous situation. You don't want to live in a constant state of fear. But simply knowing that you have the tools to save your own life—and more specifically, that you have the power to use these tools—can dramatically impact your ability to survive a potentially violent encounter.

YOUR HISTORY AS PREY

There's a saying that wildlife biologists use to differentiate between predators and prey: "Eyes in the front—I like to hunt. Eyes on the side—I like to hide."

Your eyes aren't on the sides of your head. You're no soft bunny or squirming fish. Humans are designed as predators. That means you were also born with the tools to tap into this power to do damage to another human when necessary. You just have to give yourself permission to reconnect with these innate tools when the situation warrants it.

Throughout this book, I will share the many, many ways that you can make better choices that will steer you clear of dangerous situations, whether you're at the ATM, in a nightclub, or simply driving down the street. By far the best way to save your own life is to *avoid putting it in danger in the first place*—and I will show you dozens of ways to do just that.

But I also recognize that you probably have not come to this book as a blank slate—chances are that something bad has already happened to you. Whether it was physical violence, emotional abuse, or a shaky feeling that you narrowly escaped a creepy guy on a dark street, you may have had an experience that left a lasting mark on your psyche. By taking a look at your history, we'll examine how your prior run-ins with predators may have affected your self-image so you can work toward building your confidence and empowering yourself to live a safer, freer existence.

I'll introduce you to the very ugly world of violence, and the only thing that actually works against it—causing injury. Although unpleasant, it's imperative that I do so, because most of us are completely unfamiliar with this stark reality. Let me assure you, though: The moment you experience violence, you'll *never* ignore your instincts again—*ever*. Experiencing it (or even narrowly escaping it) is learning the hard way, and I hope that never happens to you.

The more I can show you about how a predator operates, the better you'll be at avoiding the deadly games they play.

ALWAYS TRUST YOUR INSTINCTS

Marta and her husband, Jeff, took a trip to Turkey. Both are highly educated and well traveled, and neither would strike you as a typical victim if you met them. In fact, Jeff is a *big* man—he stands six foot eight and has the physique of an NFL linebacker. Their guide warned them about walking around Ankara by themselves, but the city seemed completely safe, with lots of American tourists.

After about an hour of relaxed sightseeing, Jeff spotted a local bazaar that another tourist had mentioned to him the previous day. They decided to have a look, and after buying a few souvenirs, they sat down to have some Turkish coffee. As they rested up from their long walk, the couple savored the many sights and sounds, snapping pictures of the various food vendors and enjoying snacks with their coffee.

Before long, two local men at the next table started up a conversation with Jeff. They expressed their fondness for the American tourists they had met, and relief that the Americans they'd met didn't seem to be prejudiced against Muslims, despite what local news programs were saying. Both men were charming, well dressed, and seemingly sincere. Still, although Marta couldn't put her finger on why, her instincts told her something wasn't right.

After ten or fifteen minutes of conversation, one of the men offered them some small cookies that looked similar to Oreos. "These cakes are famous in Ankara—people travel many miles just to taste these—you must try them!" one of the men insisted.

Marta's instincts screamed, *"Don't eat them!"* but her desire to be polite overpowered her inner radar. Marta and Jeff each ate a few cookies, which were laced with an unknown drug. The only thing that saved them was the fact that Jeff's size meant the drug didn't have a significant effect on him. He managed to fend off the two men, although he was injured in the process.

These two predators knew exactly how to manipulate social conventions. They built up a lot of social goodwill before they attacked. And Marta and Jeff ignored their instincts and assumed everyone around them was playing by the same social rules. Asocial violence uses these rules against you. As Marta

(continued on page 8)

Myths about Rape

Rape is a violent crime that is greatly misunderstood in our society. Our society harbors certain myths about rape that make it difficult for women to understand these crimes, let alone report them. The blame-the-victim stigma not only prevents women from seeking help, but also perpetuates myths that get women killed. Let's set a few to rest.

MYTH: Rape is a sexual act.

TRUTH: Rape is an act of brutal violence that has nothing to do with sex. Rape is all about power and domination and aggression. Instead of equating rape with "rough sex," think of it as being like a stabbing or a shooting. The rapist uses his penis as a weapon, just like a gun or a knife. That definitely is not sex.

MYTH: Most rapes are committed by strangers in dark alleys.

TRUTH: Four out of five rapes are committed by people the victims know.

MYTH: "Date rape" isn't "real" rape.

TRUTH: Rape is rape. Anytime a woman is forced or coerced against her will into having sex with someone, whether she just met him, has kissed him, or even married him, that is rape.

MYTH: Women get over rape pretty quickly.

TRUTH: Women can suffer physical and emotional trauma for years, even decades, after being raped.

MYTH: The only rape that "counts" is intercourse.

TRUTH: Women can be raped or sexually assaulted in dozens of sickening ways.

MYTH: Rape is not very common.

TRUTH: One woman in six will be raped in her lifetime; one in four female college students will experience a rape or attempted rape while in school.

Myth: When women get drunk or wear slutty clothes, they are asking to get raped.

TRUTH: Nothing a woman does, wears, says, or even thinks makes it okay to rape her. "No" means "no"—in every setting, in every relationship, in every encounter. Anyone who rapes a woman is a rapist, whether he's a thug with a knife in an alleyway, a frat boy with a beer bong and a roofie, or a husband who gets forceful because he thinks his wife "owes" him sex.

Forget the excuses. There are no valid reasons. Rape is rape.

recounted this nightmare scenario to me, I could sense that she would never ignore her instincts again. It could have been worse for Marta and Jeff, but they got lucky (and I never suggest betting your life on luck!).

NEVER ASSUME ANYTHING

In my training classes, I always play a particular YouTube video as an example of what asocial violence looks like. In this video, a highly trained female police officer has pulled over a man who has multiple outstanding warrants for felony offenses. The man's young daughter sits in the passenger seat, and so the officer doesn't pull out her gun. In turn, she assumes that the girl's presence will prevent the felon from becoming violent. In essence, *the officer thought she had an unspoken social agreement* with this man.

She was very wrong. In full view of his terrified daughter, the felon methodically beats the officer by throwing her to the ground and punching her nine times in the head. In the video, the commentator states that keeping a safe distance gives you more time to react to aggression. The officer was trained in what to do, but her social conditioning led her to believe that people don't attack other people in front of children, and that took precedence over her training. She could have handled the stop safely and effectively, but she allowed her sense of social decency to override her extensive police training.

This violent criminal probably assumed the officer would "play by the rules" and used that knowledge against her. If the felon had been alone, I'd bet anything that that day would have gone down much differently.

Think you'll pay attention to *your* instincts the next time your radar goes off? If so, just remember that this highly trained police officer *knew* she was dealing with a desperate, dangerous felon, and yet she *still* fell prey to thinking that because the felon's young daughter was present, he would be cooperative. She was quite mistaken, and she could have been killed because of it.

DON'T BE AFRAID TO ACT

Catherine entered the ground floor of a four-story parking lot with two friends. Their cars were parked on the first floor; hers was on the third. As they walked in, she noticed a guy who appeared to be watching them by the garage entrance. He was well dressed, but there was something creepy about him: The hair on the back of her neck stood up, her adrenaline surged, her heart rate increased, and she got a queasy feeling in her stomach. She considered asking one of her friends to walk her to her car, but then felt silly and gave the guy the benefit of the doubt. The creepy feeling faded as she justified heading to the elevator alone. "He's all the way over by the entrance. He's nowhere near me."

She got in, pushed "3," and when the door opened on her floor, the creepy guy was right there, his body inches from hers, blocking her from fleeing the elevator. For a moment she stood paralyzed, and he lunged at her. This guy wanted something— who knows what. It doesn't matter; it wasn't right. When he lunged, there was no time to ask questions.

Fortunately, Catherine had taken one of my Target Focus Training classes. Her training kicked in and she took action. She immediately identified a target on the guy (his groin) and a weapon in her own hand (her briefcase). In one fluid motion she stepped forward and smashed the briefcase with all her force into the guy's groin. He moved exactly as she had learned in class he would: He bent forward in agony, reflexively raising his chin. That involuntary reflex provided Catherine with a second target: She slammed all her body weight into his temple using a hammer fist (the balled-up pinky side). The combined force of her weight and the impact with the elevator door knocked this guy out. She had injured him twice even though he was much bigger and stronger than she was. His size hadn't mattered— her targeting had. With the guy out cold, Catherine felt safe enough to run and call security.

In an interesting twist, by the time security arrived, the guy was gone. He wasn't sitting there, nursing his injuries. So we can't know for certain what his intentions were—he never had to explain himself. Was it all a misunderstanding? We'll never know.

Catherine's immediate feeling was "Thank god I acted." Her husband had signed her up for my class, and she admits she'd never have come on her own. As with you, or any of us for that matter, violence was not something she wanted to dwell on. It was something that might happen to other people, not to her. But without training, her story might have had a very ugly ending.

Later she began questioning herself. Why hadn't she trusted her instincts, the nonverbal cues her body was giving her—the hair rising on the back of her neck, the queasy feeling that something was absolutely wrong—the moment she'd spotted the guy? Why had she put herself in danger?

Now, the question you must ask yourself is *What would I have done?*

AVOIDING VIOLENCE AT ALL COSTS

The three stories I've shared in this chapter have different details and somewhat varied outcomes, but they all share a very important theme: In each case, an otherwise smart, capable woman placed herself in unnecessary peril because she squelched her innate survival instincts in deference to her strong desire to "follow the rules" of a sane, civilized society.

A savvy, educated, well-traveled woman and her very large husband were both tricked by two criminals who used their humanity against them. A police officer with extensive training and a loaded firearm fell prey to a sociopathic criminal. A young woman with self-defense training ignored her survival instincts in the interest of giving an unknown man the benefit of the doubt. All three women survived their violent encounters (though the police officer was seriously harmed), but the real lesson is that all three physical encounters could easily have been thwarted.

EMPOWERING YOURSELF TO SURVIVE

If you're uncomfortable thinking about possibly hurting—or even killing—another person in order to survive, that's good. It means you're a socialized person. I understand your discomfort with this material.

Many women are initially horrified by the approach I teach: They worry that by learning how to think like predators, they'll somehow lose their humanity. But I look at it very differently. By understanding—and training for—encounters with the most violent members of society, you gain tremendous appreciation and respect for how far we've actually come as a civilized society. Because, make no mistake, we all have the innate ability to harm one another.

The following exercise may make this learning process more palatable for you. Think of someone you love more than anyone on the planet: Maybe it's your daughter, your spouse, or your mom. Next, picture a violent sociopath with a knife against her throat. Or trying to pull her into a car. Or coming in through her bedroom window at night.

What does this do to you? What feelings sweep across your body?

Is it the sense that you could handle the situation by over-powering this violent attacker? Could you save your loved one if it all depended on you?

The truth is, you probably could. After all, it's done all the time. Mothers lift cars off young children. Sisters jump in front of bullets. Friends jump into icy rivers. Our bodies are capable of tremendous physical feats when necessary.

But the bigger point I'm trying to make is that you don't even need to summon physical strength in order to save your own life, or that of a loved one. I can teach you how to bypass that eventuality altogether by avoiding an attack to begin with. All you really need to survive the unthinkable is the *strength of will to do it*.

If someone were threatening your kid or your baby sister, you wouldn't give a second thought to being judgmental, would you? Hell, no! You'd attack first and ask questions later. I want you to key in to that protective impulse—the one that gets your blood pumping when you think about a loved one facing imminent danger—but I want you to direct this toward *yourself*.

Many women are nurturers who put themselves last. But protecting yourself is the most important nurturing you can do. It's like putting your oxygen mask on first before helping others with theirs—it's not selfish, it's critical. Self-defense, especially for women, can present tough psychological hurdles, but this book will help you learn how to tap in to your existing radar to avoid the unthinkable at all costs. And if you do ever need to defend yourself, it'll also teach you how to do it bravely, confidently, and successfully. Are you ready?

CHAPTER TWO

HOW PREDATORS THINK

Your biggest problem as a woman is not that you may be smaller or weaker than a typical sociopathic criminal. It's not that you likely never have taken self-defense training (in fact, that's probably a plus, since many "self-defense" classes don't teach you how to defend yourself at all). Your biggest obstacle is that you want to play by the rules. This isn't a character flaw—it simply means that you're sane. You're civilized. Your humanity is intact. You've got empathy. The rules you play by are really quite good. They've done a lot for us over the generations— we humans couldn't have gotten as far as we have without a set of rules to help us all work together peacefully and cooperatively.

The problem is, the predators in our society look at life quite a bit differently.

SOCIOPATHS ARE REAL

"Sociopathy" is a broad term that covers the behavior of everyone from people with personality disorders to people who are psychotic. The technical definition isn't critical for this discussion, though. What really matters is that a sociopath's brain doesn't function the same way as the brains of the normal, civilized people you meet at work, next door, or at the gym.

What's the main characteristic of a sociopath? A complete lack of regard for morality and accepted social behavior. This means that a sociopath won't abide by the rules of fair play, and there's a good chance he won't even give them a passing thought. Make no mistake: This guy will not be worried about pulling dirty tricks, not playing fair, or shoving a knife through your eye. He has one thing in mind, and the ends justify the means—even if the "ends" are nothing more than the ten bucks in your wallet or soothing his savage pride.

Quite simply, a sociopath is not operating with the same set of social beliefs that you are. You are a well-adjusted, socialized person. Deep down, you believe that there's a way to resolve problems without anyone getting hurt. A sociopath doesn't.

As social, sane people, we tend to think of violence in social terms—either by framing everything as the schoolyard David and Goliath or by thinking that if we take our social conventions with us into the world, we can somehow rely on our humanity and therefore not reduce ourselves to the criminal level.

VIOLENCE HAPPENS FASTER THAN YOU THINK

We tend to think of violence as an escalating continuum: If a man yells at you, you can yell at him. If he pushes you, then you can push him. If he throws a punch, then you can throw one back. We also believe that the worst kind of violence, that which results in death, happens somewhere out there, at the end of this progression, if it gets pushed far enough.

The problem is that it is not necessary to "ramp up" or walk through all these various steps to get to serious, crippling injury or death. It's possible to punch someone in the throat or stab them in the neck at any time, in all places. This is what the criminal sociopath knows.

Can someone escalate through all the steps and whip themselves into a blind rage that ends in a killing? Yes, absolutely. But what the criminal sociopath knows is that he can get there instantaneously. He can go from smiling and shrugging to stabbing in the same amount of time it takes him to reach into his pocket. But remember, when it's absolutely necessary, so can you.

Violence is always available; you just have to be willing to do it. You can swing the tool of violence whenever you wish, even at a moment's notice. And this is exactly what you must do to survive in the face of asocial violence. Later in the book I'll go into more detail about using this tool, but for now, all that's important is that you gain some insight into the sociopath's warped way of thinking.

USING VIOLENCE AS POWER

The reason thugs use violence and get away with it certainly isn't because they're smarter. It isn't even that they're stronger—many people who get beaten up and robbed on the streets every day are fitter and stronger than their assailants. The reason muggers win is that they have a very powerful mind-set: They know what they want, and they know that if they use every violent means at their disposal, they'll get it.

They know that:

⬧ If they pull out a knife, you're going to get scared.

⬧ If they put a gun to your head, you're going to freeze.

⬧ If they threaten to kill you, you'll give them anything they demand.

They understand how to use violence to bring about the outcome they want to achieve. Am I advocating that same approach? No. Learning how to use violence doesn't turn you into a criminal; it just changes the balance of power. When you are skilled in the use of this simple mind-set, a threat from a violent person won't cause you to suffer pain, loss, or even death; instead, you will be able to cause serious injury to the attacker that results in his complete incapacitation. You'll understand that if you injure a man in a certain way, you can precisely predict the result.

Instead of letting doubt prevent you from taking action, you'll have the confidence to make the split-second decisions you need to in order to stay alive during the most stressful seconds of your life. When you've undergone this sort of training, you'll have power—the power to protect yourself and those you love.

ANTISOCIAL AGGRESSION VERSUS ASOCIAL VIOLENCE

Think about a bar fight. Even if you've never been directly involved in one, you've probably seen a bunch of drunk guys trying to establish their territory. It looks and sounds like a bunch of apes thumping their chests and baring their teeth because it's a *display* meant to be seen and heard by all those present. The participants have no intention of seriously injuring each other; in fact, if you interrupted and offered them handguns to shoot each other with, they'd probably think you were insane.

Asocial violence is brutally streamlined and economical by comparison. It starts quietly, suddenly, and unmistakably. It's knocking a man down and kicking him to death. It's one person beating another with a tire iron until he stops moving. It's stabbing someone a dozen times. It's pulling a gun and firing round after round into him until he goes down and then stepping in close to make sure the last two bullets go through his brain.

Because you're a sane, socialized person, images like this may make you physically ill. That's because you recognize them for what they are: asocial. They involve the breakdown of everything we humans hold dear, the absence of our favorite construct, the very fabric of society itself. It's an awful place where there's no such thing as a "fair fight" or honor. It's the place where there are no rules and anything goes. It's the place where people kill and get killed.

So how do you know whether you're dealing with antisocial aggression or asocial violence? Once you understand the difference between the two, it's really as easy as telling a peacock from a tiger. One involves posturing and ego; the other is all about survival. The big problem arises when we confuse the two—when we don't know the difference between competition and destruction, between antisocial and asocial violence.

The violence that comes from social posturing is avoidable; it is often loud, dramatic, and instantly recognizable. You see it coming. And that means you can dodge it if you wish to.

If you don't choose to (or cannot) leave, these sorts of problems can be handled with the social tools we're all familiar with. We've all tried to talk our way out of an uncomfortable situation with a co-worker or negotiated with an unreasonable salesperson. We all know how to calm someone down. We all know how to capitulate. We also know how to add fuel to the fire and turn an argument into a shouting match, or a shouting match into a fistfight.

The important point is that in most social situations, you have a choice.

Antisocial aggression is also eminently survivable. The typical goal in a bar fight, for example, usually isn't to kill anyone; it's to dominate another person or prove one's manhood. Does this mean you can't be killed in a bar fight? Of course not. But the typical Saturday night punch-out doesn't often result in death, and most of those fatalities are accidental. You can get killed in a bar fight, or an argument over a parking space, or any other trivial social confrontation. It's just highly unlikely.

Asocial violence, on the other hand, cannot be handled with social tools and is far less survivable. Negotiating with a serial killer is like arguing with a bullet: If it's coming your way, words are not going to deflect it. If someone has decided to stab you to death, capitulation only makes their work easier. As we discussed in the previous chapter, this is the kind of violence you must try at all costs to avoid altogether.

WHEN TO CHOOSE VIOLENCE

If you listen to people recount their experiences with violence, you'll quickly find that they fall into two distinct groups: those who have survived a truly life-or-death confrontation and those who participated in violence as a kind of sport or game.

The first group will rarely talk about the subject. When they do choose to share the experience, you'll notice that they are usually brutally honest, and almost always emphasize the fear they experienced. They make it clear that they were forced into action because they had no acceptable alternative. You'll never hear them gloat over surviving the experience, and though they may have acted heroically, they typically don't see it that way. They see themselves as fortunate to have survived, and they hope never to be in that situation again.

People who involve themselves in antisocial aggression, on the other hand, often revel in retelling how they "kicked his ass." You'll find yourself sitting through a play-by-play and listening to trash talk about the other party. These people also give the impression that they're ready to participate again should they ever be called upon to defend their reputation, a parking spot, or a spilled drink after happy hour.

Why the different responses? The first group came in contact with the ultimate specter: unavoidable life-or-death violence. No choice, no retreat, simply fight or die. In other words, the situation wasn't fun. They dealt with it and moved on.

The second group *chose* violence. They took a situation that was not life threatening and chose to respond with violence. These people enjoyed using violence to gain dominance. It was produced by a base human desire to exert control over another person's place in the pecking order. Of course, that doesn't mean the other guy wasn't "asking for it," so to speak, or that the situation couldn't have escalated into a life-or-death situation. But in this case, using violence as a response was a deliberate choice.

People choose to use violence when they allow their egos to dictate the situation. That's why a victory is enjoyable—it's an ego boost. The unavoidable use of violence produces a very different outcome: the desire not to participate in it ever again.

KEY DIFFERENCES BETWEEN ANTISOCIAL AGGRESSION AND ASOCIAL VIOLENCE

Antisocial Aggression	Asocial Violence
■ Can be resolved by using social skills	■ Is unaffected by social skills
■ Is avoidable	■ Requires decisive action to counter
■ Is survivable	■ Is often lethal

Raw violence is not something I wish on anyone, but I teach its use and methodology because there may be a time when you need that knowledge desperately. I believe you can't have enough knowledge of the subject. And quite frankly, the more competent you get at understanding all types of violence, the less likely you are to encounter it, or to waste your time choosing it to resolve a conflict in a social situation.

ARE YOU LIVING IN REALITY?

I like to use the 1999 blockbuster film *The Matrix* as an apt analogy for discussing antisocial aggression and asocial violence. If you haven't seen it, the film takes place in a future where "reality" as perceived by most people isn't real at all, but rather a simulation (called the Matrix) created by intelligent machines to pacify the human population, whose body heat and electrical activity are used as sources of energy. A computer programmer named Neo becomes aware of this and is drawn into a human uprising against the machines, joining others who have been liberated from the Matrix into reality.

One memorable scene involves a meeting between Neo and Morpheus, a leader of the rebellion. Morpheus offers Neo a choice between two pills: a blue one and a red one. If Neo chooses the blue pill, Morpheus explains, he will wake up in his bed and forget about everything that has happened. If he takes the red one, he will see reality, or, as Morpheus puts it, "see how far the rabbit hole goes."

One of my clients, Lisa, is a super-successful real estate agent based in New York City. She is petite physically, but it was immediately obvious to me that she had no problem holding her own—what Lisa lacked in stature, she more than made up for with attitude, body language, and negotiation skills. She was truly a force to be reckoned with. After describing some of the key features of my self-protection system to her, I detected a palpable sense of disdain.

"You know what?" Lisa cut in. "I think most women just don't get how simple it is to deal with aggressive men, but I'll tell you something—I grew up with four brothers, and I cut my teeth in an industry that chews most women up in less than two years. I think people overdo this whole self-defense thing."

I could sense it would be a struggle to get her to understand my philosophy. But the conversation suddenly took a surprising turn for both of us.

"I'll give you a quick example," Lisa continued. "Last Friday night I went out with a friend for drinks. Paula is a great girl, but she doesn't know how to handle men at all. For several months now, she's had this 'stalker'—a guy she met on a date once, who for whatever reason just couldn't take no for an answer. I'm not even kidding, just as she's telling me this, sure enough, she notices this idiot outside the bar!"

I wondered how all this was supposed to relate to life-or-death scenarios. Lisa continued: "I decided this was a learning opportunity for Paula. I got up, walked right out the door, put my finger right to his nose, and told him in language that even he could understand that this was his last little stalking episode and that if he didn't leave immediately, I was gonna make him regret the day he was born."

A smirk flashed across Lisa's face as she continued: "Sure enough, he basically wet his pants, which I knew he would—I've dealt with guys like this for years. Paula has never heard from the guy since then, and I think she really learned something that night—at least I hope she did."

As Lisa basked in the delight of recounting her "conquest," I quickly pulled out my laptop to show her a video of another male-female encounter that took place in Rome at a train station about five years ago. On that night, a man made a lewd comment to a nearby woman, who decided, as Lisa had, to set this guy straight. As Lisa watched the video, her face suddenly went ashen as the Italian woman walked over to the man and put her finger to his nose in *exactly* the same way Lisa had described a few moments earlier. Without a word, the man balled up his fist and unceremoniously smashed the woman straight in the face, knocking her to the concrete. He next grabbed her head with both hands and bounced it off the sidewalk, killing her instantly.

Judging by the look on her face, it was clear to me that Lisa had never seen real violence before. Sure, she had had plenty of experience with negotiation and even antisocial aggression in the workplace, and in fact she was quite skilled in dealing with those encounters. The problem was that Lisa was living in the Matrix— she thought she was dealing with reality, but the video showed her that she could have gone down a very different rabbit hole.

ARE YOU WILLING TO BET
YOUR LIFE ON LUCK?

The truth is, Lisa simply got lucky. She's lucky the guy she confronted was a civilized (although perhaps creepy and desperate) man who for the most part chose to "follow the rules." The woman in Rome wasn't so lucky—the man she confronted wasn't only rude, he was an asocial predator, and he handed her the "red pill" of reality in a quick, deadly dose.

There are two ways to take the red pill—you can either take it *before* you need it, or after it's too late. The choice is yours. I'm offering you that pill right now, and I hope you'll accept.

My friend and colleague Bill also used to live in his own version of the Matrix. One day he went for a walk with his wife, who was eight months pregnant at the time. They headed around the corner to have some lunch and a guy in a car sped by, almost hitting them both. Bill did what he normally would in that situation: flipped the guy the bird and yelled that he should watch where he's going. But that was the trigger for this guy. He stopped his vehicle, backed it up very fast, tried to hit them again, and stopped the vehicle.

Bill said, "I was completely flabbergasted, because I never expected this type of response. Not only did I have my own security to think about, but also the security of my wife and unborn child. I'm a physical person, and I can be aggressive, but that threw me completely outside of my comfort zone. Any wrong movement in a situation like that could have harmed the people that I loved the most in the world."

On that fateful day, Bill won the cosmic lottery, and he

realizes it. He now lives in the real world. When people ask if learning about violence somehow impairs their humanity or makes them less social, I use Bill's story to illustrate that just the opposite happens—Bill no longer "flips off" aggressive drivers (as many people do), because he realizes that not everyone plays by the rules. Once you step into the mind of an asocial person, you take a crucially important step into reality and become far better equipped to recognize and avoid violence, and to survive those rare instances when things go to the point of no return.

The lesson here is that there is subjective reality—the world you believe you live in, based on your experiences and observations—and then there is objective reality—the world as it *actually* is. If you've never experienced real violence—the ugly, stomach-churning, unimaginable type of event you hope never to encounter—you're still living in the former.

HOW TO RESPOND TO VIOLENCE

Once you understand the critical differences between antisocial aggression and asocial violence, you'll rarely confuse them. There's still the risk, though, that you may confuse antisocial and asocial *actions*. Antisocial actions are threatening and potentially dangerous, but there's still the possibility of dealing with them using basic social skills. Asocial actions, on the other hand, are of the "kill or be killed" variety.

Essentially, the difference hinges on the concept of *communication*. Antisocial behavior is still within the realm of communication (albeit at the bad end of it). This means that although the other guy is threatening you (by, for example, holding a knife to your neck and demanding your wallet), he's still trying, in the crudest way possible, to communicate with you. Holding a knife to your throat and shouting, "Give me your money!" is still in the realm of communication. If it were an *asocial* act, he wouldn't bother telling you what he wanted. He would simply take it.

If you use your social skills to deal with antisocial behavior, you may be able to defuse the situation and essentially "make it go away" by giving the attacker what he wants and having him honor this dubious contract by leaving. I'm sure you noticed the qualifiers I just used, and that's because there's an inherent risk in trying to reason with someone in this type of situation. There is still a possibility of resolving the situation without violence. If this is how it goes down, then it was a successful use of your social skills.

However, if at any time the situation devolves into physical violence, it would then be in the realm of asocial violence. In this category, there is no communication—only action. The goal is not to continue dialogue, but to end the interaction.

The only way to gain control of this situation is for you to be the one successfully using the tool of violence. The only way to guarantee success is to inflict an objective injury on your attacker and to continue to do so until he is nonfunctional (we'll cover this in detail in later chapters).

There are no gray areas. If you have the choice to respond with violence, then that situation is antisocial. When you have no choice, then it is asocial. In other words, if it's fight or die, you're dealing with asocial violence.

WELCOME TO REALITY

I hope you'll realize that although facing the reality of violence head-on can be scary, it also offers a refreshing, even positive perspective. First, being able to distinguish between antisocial aggression and asocial violence is very empowering, because it specifically dictates what your options are and what tools you'll need to get away safely. Second, it's probably evident by now that most violence you're likely to encounter is antisocial in nature, and as we discussed in Chapter One, as a woman, you've got great tools to use in detecting it and, even if you don't detect it, protecting yourself with a variety of communication skills.

In those rare, "unimaginable" moments when you find yourself facing true asocial violence, you can still emerge with your life intact. In the following chapters, I'll put you on an even playing field with even the most dangerous criminals by teaching you exactly how they use violence to achieve their savage ends. I know we're moving into uncomfortable territory here, but stay with me—you can do this. Actually, anyone can. You just need to know what to do and have the will to do it.

Chapter Three

YOUR MOST POWERFUL WEAPON

Imagine that you've fallen into a pool. What's your first instinct? Would you let yourself sink underwater and wait for a lifeguard to come get you? Or would you know what to do to save your own life?

Obviously, you would swim! Using the principles I'm teaching you in this book to safeguard your well-being is no different from learning to swim (which you should think of doing as a precaution against drowning). Once you've learned the basics, you're set. You won't feel anxious about pools; you won't keep your fingers crossed at night and hope to avoid them. You'll have attained basic competency in a life skill that gives you the security of knowing that if you fall in a pool, you'll be able to swim. You may never compete in the Olympics, but then, you don't need a gold medal to keep your head above water.

GET TO KNOW YOUR INTUITION

Most people don't apply this same commonsense approach toward their safety on dry land. We live in a society that seems safe on the surface, so no one wants to think about what lies underneath—unless they are forced to. People are afraid of violence. They're afraid of experiencing it, so much so that many people have *no response at all* when they do encounter it. They fall into the pool and they sink. I know this because many of my clients come to me after something bad has already happened to them. They tell me how they "froze" or how their "mind went blank." Often by sheer luck, these people survived. But I don't want you to put your personal safety in the hands of luck. I want you to take that power into your own hands, and that starts with trusting yourself and your instincts.

As a woman, you possess the world's most powerful predator detection system: your female intuition. Yet most women spend much of their lives oblivious to its power. Serious apprehension in your gut—that queasy "oh my god" feeling—is the result of a primitive part of your brain reading and interpreting danger signals. That could be one of the signals that let you know your attacker is lethal.

One of the most common questions I hear is "How will I know when it's a real threat, and really time to act?" I'm not going to be with you at that moment. Only you will be able to decide if a real threat exists. That's why, before you learn the physical techniques of self-protection, your task is to reacquaint yourself with and to learn to trust and *use* your gut instincts—your strongest and most reliable weapons in the fight against predators.

WHAT WOULD YOU DO?

When was the last time you put a knife to someone's neck and demanded their watch? You've never done this? Then you don't think like a predator. That's a good thing, surely. But it also illustrates a vital point—someone who would do such a thing doesn't think like you. They aren't playing by the same societal rules you are, and so you can't react as if they are.

You have probably considered one or more of the following:

⋄ If I am ever attacked, I will just try to reason with them and give them what they want—surely they will go away.

⋄ If I am attacked, I will scream at the top of my lungs and *never* get in a car with them.

⋄ If I am attacked, I will pretend that my boyfriend is on the phone with me. I always carry my cell phone in my hand for that very purpose.

⋄ I won't be attacked, because I carry pepper spray in my purse.

⋄ I have no idea what I would do if I was attacked.

You have probably been told that your options are to defend yourself by screaming to attract attention, running away, talking him down, or pretending you have a male friend who's just out of sight. But during a truly violent encounter, you have only about five seconds to act, and the things mentioned above won't save your life against a predator. Real-life danger is not an old-fashioned melodrama, with you being tied to railroad tracks as a train is coming and

Life or Death

When it comes to asocial violence, you must do one of three things: render your attacker incapacitated, unconscious, or dead. Could you do this if your life depended on it?

Consider this scenario: A woman is putting away groceries in the kitchen. She doesn't notice that the back door is open. Suddenly, an intruder approaches and grabs her around the neck, holding her in a choke position. She clutches his hands, trying to pull them away from her neck. The attacker grabs a knife that's on the counter and thrusts it into her neck. She dies.

Now consider this scenario: A woman is putting away groceries in the kitchen. She doesn't notice that the back door is open. Suddenly, an intruder approaches and grabs her around the neck, holding her in a choke position. She remembers that there's a knife on the counter, grabs it, and thrusts it into the attacker's neck. *He* dies.

The knife to the side of the neck worked both times. Which would you choose?

your only choice is to shout for help and wait (hope) for someone to rescue you. Shouting isn't going to stop the train. And you don't have time to wait for a hero. When seconds count, you need to save yourself from a physical assault.

Your primary goal is to teach yourself to listen to your intuition the first time, *before* you say good-bye to your friends.

Before you get on the elevator. Respecting your intuition strengthens it, like a muscle. If you learn to listen to your intuition the very first time it sends out a warning signal, you will not only avoid most dangerous places, but also instantly recognize and respond to the need to act if you're in a situation you couldn't avoid. You'll trust yourself, and you will take down that threat.

AN OUNCE OF PREVENTION IS WORTH A POUND OF CURE

Here's another way women have the edge over men from a survival standpoint: Studies show that women are much more likely than men to seek medical attention soon after they start feeling not quite right or notice a symptom of some kind. (Similarly, women are more likely to ask for directions *before* they get lost, as opposed to men, who often wait until the bitter end!) What's behind this phenomenon? Probably ego—most men hate to admit they are fallible or that something could be wrong with them.

Most women, on the other hand, don't take it as a sign of weakness when they need help medically or navigationally. They know that something isn't quite right and aren't afraid to speak up to make sure they're on the right track. I'd like you to ponder that for a moment and then apply it to what we're discussing in this chapter: Using your intuition is your first (and best) chance to avoid the unthinkable. As a woman, you're more likely to be hardwired for early avoidance. You win when you play to your strengths—remember that. Let's talk about some intuition-building exercises you can use to help you start valuing this critical ability.

> **When you learn to spot predatory tendencies, you strengthen your intuition.**

> **When you strengthen your intuition, you create healthy emotional and physical boundaries.**

> **When you have those boundaries, you can more easily avoid predators.**

> **And when you can't avoid predators, using the tool of violence helps you destroy them.**

In every class I teach, I ask how many of the women felt physically uncomfortable around or threatened by a man within the prior forty-eight hours. Every time, hands go up. The guys in the class are visibly shocked to learn this. As a woman, here's what might visibly shock *you*—men can go for months, even *years*, without giving a thought to their physical safety. Some try in vain to recall the last time they got shoved against a wall or had a swing taken at them.

Keep in mind, I don't ask the class whether a man put his hands on them. I ask, "When was the last time a man made you feel so uncomfortable you were glad just to get the hell away from him?" That's when the hands go up and the stories begin. Women tend to be good at recognizing creeps because they pick up on cues that many men are oblivious to. Most experts believe that women have better intuition for some key biological and evolutionary reasons. First off, women have a more highly developed ability to understand the subtle meanings behind people's body language—their gestures, expressions, and tones of voice. This skill probably developed in response to childbearing, to allow them to use nonverbal cues to determine their babies' needs. The two sides of women's brains are also better integrated, having more neural connections between the left and right hemispheres than there are in men. That makes women better able to quickly pick up on patterns and hidden meanings that men may see as random details.

TRUST YOUR GUT

Another factor at play is the huge number of neurons—a type of brain cell—that live in your gastrointestinal tract. It's not your imagination: Your "gut instinct"—that butterfly feeling you get when you're excited, or that stomach clenching that happens when you're dreading something—is actually your "second brain," as the gut is called, telling you to pay attention. Your heart also has millions of neurons, and research suggests that the heart reacts more quickly to stimulating circumstances than the brain does. Women have been proven to be better at keying in to these body sensations—so, if you can learn to trust them, you have a tremendous leg up!

Helen Fisher, PhD, a biological anthropologist at Rutgers University, also cites women's typical interest in other people as a huge asset in the development of intuition. Fisher contends that as women collect observations about, interactions with, and assessments of people, they develop a tendency she calls chunking—the ability to detect patterns (or "chunks") of behavior. Recalling these chunks in later interactions helps them quickly figure out the subtext of a situation or identify a threat without having to wade through all the details to come to the same conclusions again. If you've been abused before, you will be more highly attuned to signals of danger. The trick is not to block out that predatory experience, but rather to use it to recognize the signals, not freeze, and tap in to your specialized life skills to keep yourself safe.

SHARPENING YOUR GREATEST WEAPON

All these innate traits and tendencies are just waiting to be honed. Try some of these exercises that will help you strengthen your intuition muscle. Once you've connected with that inner warning signal, you'll be ready to move on to learning the physical techniques for self-protection—because, ultimately, it's what you do with this information that counts.

Practice people watching. At its root, your intuition is partially your subconscious's ability to recognize something your conscious thoughts haven't caught up with yet. Say you're walking down the street and out of the corner of your eye, you register that a guy is sitting in a car with the engine running— or that he's sitting in a car and the engine is not running. Your brain picks up on all those details and quickly chunks them together with other details in the environment. The better you can get at noticing small details about people and your surroundings in complex situations, the more networked information you'll have in your intuition database.

Be a part-time social scientist. Perch on a park bench or grab a seat at an outdoor café or in the food court at the mall. Watch people go by, and really look at details—what kind of shoes is he wearing? Is she wearing an appropriate coat for the weather? Is he wearing a wedding ring? How quickly is she walking? Create scenarios about where people are going, what they're shopping for, how happy they are in their relationships or in their jobs. The focus here is not to try to be accurate—you'll never know whether you are—but just to practice noticing a level of detail that might give you critical information someday.

Study facial expressions. While no one can truly read minds (yet), the ability to read people's faces can be a very useful skill when building up your database. Researchers have postulated that humans share seven basic emotions: happiness, sadness, fear, surprise, disgust, anger, and contempt. These emotions correspond to very specific facial expressions. "Microexpressions," which are these expressions when they flit involuntarily across our faces in about one-fifteenth of a second, are important clues for recognizing who's a threat. Psychologists have found that women are better at registering lightning-fast shifts in facial microexpressions. One of the most important expressions to look for is contempt, which is characterized by a sneer. Criminals often show tremendous contempt for their victims. Contempt is a feeling that comes from despising or not respecting someone. Being able to spot a look of unconscious contempt on another person's face can give you a heads-up that they don't respect you. Beyond spotting contempt to avoid danger, being able to identify others' emotions quickly is a handy life skill that greatly enhances your intuition. You can practice spotting microexpressions at Web sites such as face.paulekman.com and humintell.com.

Make it a game. I once knew a daughter of a Mafia enforcer who grew up around violence. She'd seen some pretty horrific things as a child, and she was no stranger to brutality—violence was just part of her life. I didn't have to explain the premise of my system to her; she got it right away. She had lived it. When it came time to have her own kids, she made sure they understood the basics of violence prevention from an early age. She didn't do it to scare them—she did it because, based on who they were, there was a very good chance they might encounter it at any time. But she managed to make it fun for them. Starting when they were about four years old, whenever they pulled into a bank drive-thru, she would say, "Okay, who can count all the people in the parking lot for me?" or "Who is on lookout in the front seat? How about the backseat?" This game not only served a practical purpose for her—giving her two extra sets of eyes when her back was turned—but also let her teach them the foundation of self-protection: awareness.

Meditate for ten minutes every day. This might sound a little fluffy for a self-defense expert to suggest, but developing a practice of meditation can help you stay safe for many reasons. First off, consistent meditators tend to be more attuned to details in their moment-to-moment existence. Rather than wandering around in a daze on autopilot (a predator's dream!), meditators are "present" and tend to be more connected to their senses, which are the conduits for essential information about dangerous situations. Also, meditators' brains give them greater conscious control over their instinctive emotional reactions. They're less likely to freeze up in scary situations because they are in touch with their base instinctual emotions, such as fear, but not ruled by them. Meditators practice "noticing" their thoughts and emotions in a way that gives them easy access to them all the time—a critical skill in those moments when fleeting thoughts matter.

REVIEW YOUR THREAT HISTORY

Here's an important exercise to strengthen your instincts. Scan through all the times in your life when you've felt most threatened or actually experienced violence. Pick one incident, close your eyes, put yourself back in the situation, and really study it with all your senses: What do you smell, hear, and see? What is around you? What are the most prominent physical details you can remember about the threatening person?

Now, this is the important part: What choice did you make that put you in that situation? What did you say to yourself before you did that? "It's only ten blocks. I don't need a ride/cab/friend to walk me home." "He paid for dinner, so I shouldn't be such a cold fish." Now, imagine that you'd made another choice—maybe turned down the date, or accepted the ride home, or just handed over the purse and not resisted the mugger. How might the outcome have been different?

Self-Protect Your Ride

We are a nation of solo drivers. That's bad for the environment, sure—but even worse for our security. Keep these simple safety measures in mind.

GET AN ANTI-CARJACKING SYSTEM FOR YOUR CAR: With this feature, the passenger and rear doors lock automatically as soon as you get in the car, preventing someone from jumping in while you're stopped. If your car doesn't have this feature, make locking the doors upon entry a reflexive habit.

CONSIDER SUBSCRIBING TO A NAVIGATIONAL SERVICE SUCH AS ONSTAR: These services are relatively inexpensive and usually have a "panic button" feature that sends help your way even if you become unconscious or are otherwise unable to respond.

USE YOUR A/C: Having the windows down on a sunny day is invigorating, but when you're in stop-and-go traffic or will be stopping often, roll up the windows. Leaving them open leaves you exposed.

FORGET THE WORKOUT: Many fitness experts say, "Park your car as far from the store entrance as possible to get some extra exercise!" I say, "Park as close as you can so when you're leaving the store later, laden with all your bags and digging through your purse for your keys, you're not a target!" Also, park under a light at night whenever possible, and have your keys in hand before leaving the store.

BACK IN: Whenever possible, back your car into your parking space rather than pulling in forward—you'll not only be able to leave the space quickly, but if you're parked against a wall, you'll face the rest of the parking lot, and no one will be able to sneak up behind you as you open the door.

PARK AND GET OUT: Once you've parked, don't dawdle. Make your phone calls inside the building, in the bathroom if you have to, and do your makeup and hair there, too. Anytime you're sitting in your car and it's not in gear, you're basically trapped.

BE A SMART SAMARITAN: Do your charity work off-road. Never pick up a hitchhiker or roll down your window when a stranger approaches. Don't pull over on the street to ask for directions; go to a service station instead. Don't be the one who stops to help the guy with car trouble; call the police instead. That's what *they're* there for, not you.

Repeat this exercise at least two or three times with different incidents. Do you notice any patterns? Did you avoid asking for help? Do you tend to say yes to things that make you feel uncomfortable, simply in order to avoid conflict or seeming distrustful? How could you react differently to keep yourself safe next time? Recall your last "queasy stomach" feeling. When was the last time you felt uncomfortable around a man? When that guy lingered behind you at the ATM? Or that valet was super aggressive getting your car? The "nice guy" at your yoga studio flipping out when you said you didn't want to go for coffee? Why were you scared when the conversation during your last date got weird? The way he stood so close to you, it wasn't flirting—it was something else. How about the guy at the bar who stared at you in a way that didn't feel quite right? He didn't say or do anything, but you felt relieved when your friends arrived.

These are all situations that you can realistically expect to encounter in everyday life, or may already have. And they are all potentially dangerous. They make you uncomfortable because they force you to recognize two things:

✧ Something is not quite right.

✧ I might have to fight back if he tries to hurt me.

So ask yourself again: When was the last time you felt the hair on the back of your neck stand on end? Your heart race uncontrollably? You got that stomach-clenching "this isn't right" feeling in your gut? And what did you do about it? What will you do differently next time?

YOUR MOST VALUABLE WEAPON

When my trainers ask new clients to list the weapons at their disposal, highly trained law enforcement personnel and inexperienced people give the same answers: what external weapons and objects (briefcase, umbrella, pen, etc.) they carry with them. Almost everyone fails to list their most powerful weapon: their mind. And it is a devastating weapon—in violent situations, a trained brain can quickly and easily outmaneuver brawn.

How does the brain become a weapon? When you flip your thinking from defensive to proactive. As I mentioned earlier, many self-protection classes teach women to react to an attacker's actions. This defensive thinking trains them to hesitate ("What is he going to do to me?"), lose focus (waiting to get hurt makes most people freeze), and ultimately be one step behind their attacker ("He hit me; now I can hit back"). I want you to change your thinking from defensive to reactive and to focus on targets (specific anatomical features that are vulnerable to injury), which will put you one step ahead of a potential threat.

Once you start thinking, "How will I attack this man?" rather than "What is he going to do to me?" your brain will work against his brawn. Because as big and tough as he is, if you know how to target his windpipe, he won't be bothering you for long. Having the proper reactive frame of mind before and during an attack makes all the difference between success and failure.

Right about now, if you are well adjusted, your mind is not becoming reactive so much as it is recoiling. I just told you that you'll have to cause injury to a person who is threatening you.

This feels uncomfortable—it isn't self-defense. It isn't blocking someone's punch and getting to safety. It is the opposite: It is going on the offensive to cause injury. Why would you do this?

Because unlike blocking blows and running away, the tool of violence, when used decisively, will stop an attack every time. Would you bet your life on your ability to block the punch of a man who outweighs you by a hundred pounds? Are you certain you can run as fast as you would need to after receiving such a blow? If you were, you wouldn't be reading this book. So ask yourself what matters more to you: people's opinions of you ("I can't believe she hit him first!") or your life ("I broke that guy's nose before he could hit me").

We all get complacent in our lives. We act like we're safe because we want to feel safe, even when we know inside that we're really just fooling ourselves. Some of the best lessons for protecting yourself and being aware can be learned from predators. Now that you have become aware of them, and know what to do if you encounter one, I can teach you how to use a predator's tools to protect yourself and the things that are most important to you.

UNDERSTANDING VIOLENCE DOESN'T MAKE YOU VIOLENT

A bit of reassurance may be called for: The information in this book won't turn you into a cold-blooded killer. Research shows that even among elite military forces, overall aggression decreases after they are trained properly. Soldiers become more confident and don't want to get drawn into conflicts. They are more aware of the severity of the methods they have learned, and don't want to use them unless it's absolutely necessary. They also know that those methods can kill, and they know others know them, too. They understand why it's usually wiser *not* to engage, that posturing is idiotic and solves nothing. Avoidance is better than fighting. You enter a conflict only when it's absolutely necessary, and when you can finish it.

You're a good person, and you don't want to cause injury to another person. I feel the same way. But if you find yourself in a situation where you don't have a choice, where your life is on the line, I'm here to tell you that you *can* control a bad situation from the moment you cause the first injury. You will have the confidence and willpower to injure your attacker until he is in a nonfunctional state. This means incapacitation, unconsciousness, or even death. Yes, by the end of this book, you will know how to kill someone—and that knowledge may help you save your own life.

CHAPTER FOUR

THE WILL TO SURVIVE

Here's a summary of what we've covered so far. As a woman, you have a fair chance of being attacked at some point in your life. You can hide from this fact or face it head-on. If you decide to face it head-on, the first thing to do is realize that most threats can be outright avoided by staying aware and trusting your built-in survival instincts. There are two types of threats: antisocial aggression, which can be either avoided or deflated using communication skills, and asocial violence, which is unavoidable and requires decisive action if you expect to survive. In those rare instances when a violent attack is imminent (asocial violence), there are two factors involved in your survival: *knowing* what to do (understanding where the vulnerable points on your attacker's body are and the techniques you'll need to injure these targets) and being *willing* to do it.

Simple enough, right? The surprising thing about what I teach is that it's very easy to understand and, believe it or not, very straightforward to accomplish. What's *not* so simple, however, is having the willingness to do it.

This is why it's critically important that you be *willing* to use the mechanics of violence as a survival tool when the situation calls for it. As a woman, you might be concerned that you won't have sufficient strength to fight back, but this wouldn't be your primary problem, as I'll explain very shortly. Instead, you're much more likely to be held back by your reluctance to harm someone else.

COULD YOU USE VIOLENCE TO PROTECT YOURSELF?

Why do so many women have trouble inflicting physical harm on another person? One explanation might be genetic: Males evolved to be protectors and providers—they are hardwired to hunt and kill prey and to protect their families from external threats, whether they be wild animals or other humans. Women, of course, also evolved as protectors, but in the very different way of providing their children with comfort, nurturing, and sustenance.

All of which is simply to say that the use of violence comes much more easily to men than it does to women, generally speaking. This explains why the overwhelming majority of violent sociopaths are men. With that said, however, it's important for you to know that the will or intent you'll need can in fact be learned.

If you're squeamish about using violence as a survival tool, it's probably for one of two reasons.

You're afraid. There's something more than simple civility underlying your aversion to violence. I bet that if you sat down right now and made yourself a list of the top ten reasons you don't want to be involved in a violent encounter, most of them would come from the same source: fear. As we've discussed, it's perfectly normal to be afraid of violence. But you can't let your fear prevent you from acting to ensure your own survival.

You may assume that as a large, strong, highly trained man, I can't relate to the fear that envelops you when you consider the prospect of being violently attacked. The truth is, I absolutely can empathize with you, because I understand the true nature of violence. Yes, I'm strong and trained to deal with violence, but I'm also acutely aware of how vulnerable I am. If even a small, relatively weak woman struck me in the eye or throat or groin (or another of the vulnerable targets I'll share with you shortly), I'd be in big trouble.

As Target Focus Training master instructor Chris Ranck-Buhr stated, "Women are precisely as capable as men at causing injury; when a thumb goes into an eye socket, the universe doesn't stop everything and check if the cells in the thumb have XY or XX chromosomes before deciding if the forces exerted are enough to destroy the eyeball. Either the forces exceed the elasticity of the tissue or they don't. Male vs. female is not a part of that equation."

You feel that using violence lessens your humanity. If this is a concern for you, don't be surprised or concerned—it simply means that you're sane and well socialized. However, are your moral convictions against killing so strong that you'd allow a

Learn from Survivors

Here's some homework for you: Check out the program
I Survived . . . on the Biography Channel. The show features survivors explaining, in their own words and without
dramatic reenactments, how they overcame life-threatening
situations. Some of the stories are from people who were
injured in unfortunate accidents, attacked by animals,
or caught in natural disasters such as floods or fires, but
many others relate robberies, rapes, kidnappings, and
other violent situations.

As you watch the program, I'd like you to involve yourself in two ways:

First, as you watch each story unfold, compare the victim's responses to the recommendations you're reading in
this book. Did the person survive out of sheer luck (which
does sometimes happen) or because they took decisive
action? Put yourself in their position and consider how you
might handle the same situation.

Then, when the victim explains why they thought
they survived their particular ordeal, notice how often
(even in stories about people facing nonhuman threats)
they say something along the lines of "I survived because
I wasn't ready to die—I took the necessary action to
save myself." In essence, what they're saying is that they
had the *will* to survive, despite experiencing enormous
fear and uncertainty.

deranged sociopath to kill you or your child? No, of course not. Your survival depends on it.

Hopefully, by now you've come to realize that I don't endorse the use of violence in the way a criminal sociopath would use it. Violence should never be used to get what you want unless that's trying to survive a violent attack, and in all situations it's an absolute last resort.

But when it becomes your *only* option, you have to be ready to act decisively.

People are afraid of violence. They're afraid of experiencing it, and they're afraid of doing it. If you go into a room full of people and start talking about crushing windpipes, they're going to keep their distance from you. We live in a society that's safe on the surface, but violence does happen—and no one wants to think about it happening to them.

But of course, sometimes it does happen, and if you ever encounter it, there's only one way to survive it. And in order to do that, you have to accept the use of violence as a tool—not good or evil in and of itself, but a tool that can be used for good or evil depending on who gets ahold of it and how they're swinging it.

In other words, violence takes on the moral context of the user—but only after the fact. Beating someone to death with a metal pipe can be murder in one instance and justified homicide in another—but in both cases, someone beat someone else to death. Knowing how to do it doesn't make you a bad person. Using that knowledge to bully, intimidate, injure, or kill others is *an entirely different thing* from using that knowledge to protect yourself and your family when the situation requires it.

DOES THIS BOOK ADVOCATE
EXCESSIVE VIOLENCE?

When cornered, most people are willing to accept, at least on an intellectual level, that violence can come in handy. If you say to someone, "I know self-defense," you'll get a very different reaction than you will if you say, "I know how to kill people." But the first is an empty, generic statement, and in a real life-or-death encounter with asocial violence, it's not going to save your life.

Now, I'm not saying you should go around bragging about knowing how to kill people—that's irresponsible and inappropriate. But you should know how to do it, and you shouldn't be ashamed of having that knowledge.

Civilized society really prefers that you meet force with like force: If he pushes, you're allowed to push; if he slaps and chokes you, you're allowed to slap and choke back. And if he tries to kill you, you're allowed to fight back to the death. That's fine—as long as he doesn't get the "kill" idea before you do. Of course, if he just slaps you and you break his nose, some people will call that "excessive" violence. To me, this kind of criticism is a fundamental misunderstanding of violence itself. Why was it excessive? Because he didn't break your nose first?

When faced with dangerous violence, you must act quickly and effectively to incapacitate your attacker before he hurts you. It's the only way to stop him from continuing to harm you.

ISN'T THIS INFORMATION DANGEROUS?

One of the objections I most commonly hear from people is "What if criminals get ahold of this information? Isn't it dangerous to give them access to the information they need to kill and maim other people?"

This would be an excellent objection except for one thing: They *already know* how to use violence to get what they want!

Do they know all the principles and methods included in this book? No. But they have no problem with using violence to get what they want, and they know the critical factor that makes violence work: intent.

As I've stated numerous times in my newsletters, live trainings, and DVDs—to use violence successfully, you really don't need physical training, but you *must* have intent. If you have years of "training" and no intent, you'll lose every time. *Every* time. In general, criminals don't waste time learning to use their tools better—they rely on intent alone.

The system I've developed and refined over the years has created a fundamental change in the way my clients—all of them good people—go about protecting themselves. At first, for some, the information is uncomfortable, even shocking. But it rings true. My job is not to worry that the criminals will get ahold of this info, but to worry that good people won't. They are the ones who truly need this program. All a criminal would likely do is look at it and nod his head in agreement.

ACTING IN THE FACE OF FEAR

For far too long, so-called self-defense fallacies have held sway while common criminals have exploited fear and ignorance. The simple principles that govern the effective use of violence as a survival tool are well known to them, but much less familiar to law-abiding, successfully socialized citizens. Remember these simple facts:

You *can* take decisive action in the face of fear. The first reaction in any violent situation is the most primal emotion, fear. When a man steps out of the shadows holding a knife or an intruder pulls open the curtain in your shower, your adrenaline immediately starts pumping and your heart beats faster. These are natural reactions that cannot be avoided—nor should they be. They are part of the fight-or-flight survival response that allows you to focus completely on destroying your enemy or getting the hell out of there.

Many people fear that they will be overwhelmed by fight-or-flight impulses and behave irrationally or "freeze up" and be incapable of acting.

Once you know how to swim in the pool of violence, however, your reaction will be slightly different. You will still experience the biological fear response, but it will be tempered by knowing what to do next. Instead of being shocked and frightened and believing you have no choice but to submit, you'll do what you've been trained to do. If that training taught you to wait and see or to get ready, you may already have lost. If, however, that training taught you to use violence—to cause injury—then that's what you'll do.

Violence is available to everyone. Believe it or not, you are a predator with stereoscopic vision that allows you to hunt prey and teeth capable of ripping and tearing flesh. You are a member of the only species that has made an art of war. The average human body is an awesome engine of destruction driven by one of the most dangerous things in the known universe: a human brain. Start thinking of yourself as a survival machine, the descendant of winners—your ancestors didn't get you here by giving up and lying down. They made the losers do that. Violence is your birthright.

In general, the one *doing* the violence (not the one receiving it) tends to prevail. Effectively used violence results in one person injuring another. While all violent acts have injury in common, they also share another trait: At the end, the person walking away is typically the one who initiated it.

THINK MECHANICALLY, NOT EMOTIONALLY

People, especially women, struggle with the concept of violent intent for a number of reasons. Most of us (thankfully) have a strong, natural disinclination toward violence. Not wanting to hurt people is admirable, healthy, sane, and "normal," but ultimately it's also an impediment to survival in the face of antisocial behavior. Sociopaths don't have superior training, skill, size, strength, or speed—if they did, your chances would be nil in a life-or-death encounter. Their primary advantage over you is that they are *willing* to kill, and they know their victims aren't. It's that simple.

We also worry about what the other person will do if we strike. Badly injured people are completely helpless. Ask anyone who's ever been decked in the belly or face multiple times. That first injury transforms a fully functional person into a gagging sack of flesh, and repeated injuries leave a person down on the ground. I drill this truth into my clients time and time again: *Injured people can't hurt you, and they can't kill you.* In an asocial situation, that's all that matters. What's he going to do if you strike first? He going to break and behave like a pained, injured person in the throes of a reflexive retreat (more on that later). And you're going to put him there.

In any violent conflict there's going to be, by definition, at least one person inflicting harm on another. Be the one who's inflicting the pain. Decide that it will be you from now on. That out there, it will always be your turn. If you have to think in terms of there being an "attacker," then it must be you. Choosing to put yourself in second place is not the best strategy for winning, no matter how much we may love an underdog. In a fair fight or a contest, the underdog could be the hero. With real violence, the underdog could wind up dead.

If the idea of killing someone truly bothers you, remember: Empathizing with a dead man at his funeral is sane and normal. Empathizing with him when he's lunging at you means it might be *your* funeral. In a violent conflict, there is no room for empathy. You must replace emotional and ethical rationales with pure survival instinct.

Bottom line: Decide who should remain standing. Is it you, or is it him?

PERMISSION TO SURVIVE

In a purely technical sense, violence is really, really easy. Humans are predators, and physically, we're built for killing. Performing a violent act is as easy as striking someone in the

A Coroner's Perspective on Violence

P. Michael Murphy is the coroner for Clark County, Nevada. During his typical workweek, Murphy told me, he examines bodies showing defensive wounds incurred as these victims fought back during the violent attacks that killed them. Some bodies have none of these defensive wounds, though, leading him to believe that those victims were so surprised by the attacks that they had no time to react, or no reaction at all.

Murphy related that, in his opinion, if you are attacked, you should *commit* to whatever you decide to do. If you decide to defend yourself in a life-threatening situation, don't do it halfheartedly. Flailing at someone might leave DNA under your fingernails, but it won't save your life. In his view, women should capitulate *only* to gain access to vulnerable targets such as the groin, eyeballs, etc. The two most incapacitating injuries he sees in victims: strangulation and blows to the head.

The bottom line is this: Cops see the people who were successful at defending themselves; coroners see those who weren't.

groin. You strike as hard as you can, he goes down, and it's over so fast you won't even have time to break a sweat.

The hard part is giving yourself permission to be brutal. Giving yourself permission to survive. You must choose whether you prefer living with the guilt of seriously damaging or killing another human being, or giving up your own life so a sociopath can rummage through your purse.

Thinking that violence is difficult (so you don't have to face the question of intent) is akin to thinking that you have to swim differently in the deep end than you do in the shallow end. Mechanically, it's the same—swimming is swimming—so the difference is all in your perception. In the shallow end, you can touch bottom and save yourself from drowning by standing up. In the deep end, you're on your own—it's sink or swim.

Violent intent—your willingness to cause injury, your drive to get it done—is completely up to you. You need to start thinking about it now, and let go of the reasons it makes you uncomfortable or unsure. Practice by thinking about situations where you must choose between hurting another person and saving your own life. Remind yourself of how much you have to lose if you don't act first. And empower yourself with the knowledge that if you had to, you could stomp on the throat of a screaming man.

"INTENT" MEANS AS HARD AS YOU CAN

Violent intent is what makes people scary. It's what you instinctively fear in a criminal. It's behavior society prohibits in domesticated humans. But what is it, exactly?

"Intent" is a single-minded, goal-oriented focus

In terms of violence, "intent" means being focused on injuring another person to the exclusion of all else: From the moment you perceive a threat until the moment the threat is gone, all you care about is causing injury. From the moment he pulls up his shirt to show you a gun or from the moment you hit the ground face-first, you must be on a self-protective mission to locate any available targets. Find your targets and strike them systematically, never stopping, never hesitating until you are able to place an injury. And once you do place an injury, continue to strike until he physiologically buckles and is unable to come after you or hurt you. "Intent" is about what you are going to force him to do. "Intent" is making violence one-sided as quickly as possible and keeping it that way.

It's not an emotional state—you're not enraged or Hulked out or seeing red. It's just that, of all the myriad things you can do, you pick one (injuring) and pursue it to the exclusion of all else, over and over again. One target, one injury. Repeat until continuing is no longer necessary.

"Intent" is how hard you swing the bat

Intent is a self-realizing prophecy that cuts both ways: If you think you can do it, you will; if you think you can't, you won't.

If I ask you to kick a soccer ball, how hard you kick it will depend on what you expect to happen. If you believe that the ball is filled with lead, then you'll expect it to hurt and won't kick it as hard as you can. In fact, you'll be very reluctant to kick it at all, and your performance will reflect that reluctance. In a word, it'll suck.

If, on the other hand, I tell you that if you don't kick the ball over the fence I'm going to shoot you in the head, your performance will suffer even more. Your preoccupation with a negative outcome will sabotage your efforts. Your mind will not be focused on the task at hand. You'll be worried about dying while simultaneously trying to succeed.

Focus on reality as it stands, not on all possible outcomes. Thinking that there's nothing you can do, or that you cannot injure him, or that you're going to die are all outright lies until they are proven true. I call this "feeding the phantoms." Why put your efforts into ensuring your own defeat? It does nothing to help you shape the reality you want. In violence, the reality you want is the one where he's injured. Everything you do must get you there by the shortest possible route. To consider failure is to aid in your own destruction.

"Intent" is how much of yourself you'll put into getting it done

Here's a compelling fact that I like to bring up at training seminars: The one thing that all survivors have in common is that they believed they could survive. The circumstances are immaterial; it could be a crash, drowning, fire, wilderness, or violence. Survivors report time and time again that when they reached the final decision point—"Am I going to live or die?"—they all unequivocally, steadfastly chose to live. They believed they could. I've never heard a survivor say, "And then I quit and waited to die." (Okay, to be fair, I have heard some say that, but they were saved by others who refused to give up.)

Survivors believe they can alter the outcome.

So, back to the soccer ball. If I hand it to you so you can feel how light and kickable it is and then tell you that our goal for this training session is to see how far you can kick it, then you are free to work on the mechanics of running up and kicking it with your whole being. This is what I'm attempting to do in this book. Only instead of kicking soccer balls, we're kicking people in the groin.

If you show up with the false assumption that, even though you felt the ball and it was indeed light and bouncy, it will still hurt when you kick it, or that you are incapable of kicking it very far, then anything I do to train you is for naught. You sabotaged yourself before you even set foot on the pitch. Negative expectations lead to diminished results. Believing you can do it, expecting to get it done, gets you what you want.

Intent comes down to wanting to cause an injury in order to guarantee your own survival. Focus your mind in that direction, on that single vulnerable target, and your body will follow suit. It takes focus to walk away alive.

All because you have the simple belief that you can do it— you can protect yourself.

In the following chapters, we'll deal with the *mechanics* of violence—the science of causing injury. I'll teach you how to locate the most vulnerable points on the human body and how to injure them with simple but effective attacks that work even when you're in a blind panic. Although this material will almost certainly make you uncomfortable, the reward you'll receive is more gratifying than you might imagine: true peace of mind.

CHAPTER FIVE

THE ENGINE
OF VIOLENCE

omen who've already faced a violent attack "get it"; they understand the reality of violence, and some escaped almost certain death by injuring their attackers. Hindsight is twenty-twenty, as the saying goes.

Then there are the women who haven't encountered true violence themselves, but know someone who has and therefore can appreciate the gravity of the situation. When you know someone who's been violently attacked, it's natural to put yourself in their shoes and wonder, "What would I have done?"

Some women, whether they've experienced violence or not, can accept on a purely analytical level that the only way to stop an attacker intent on causing harm is to render him nonfunctional by injuring him.

Finally, many women who are mothers find that the

protective maternal instinct provides the motivation necessary to accept the reality of violence and learn how to protect themselves and their children should it someday be necessary.

Please remember that the use of violence is a survival tool to be used when you're faced with an asocial predator who is determined to harm or kill you. You couldn't avoid it, you can't talk your way out of it, and oh shit, here he comes . . . it's either him or you. Either he renders you nonfunctional by injuring you, or you render *him* nonfunctional by injuring him. It's exactly that simple. One or the other.

Perhaps you'll appreciate my now-famous quote: "Violence is rarely the answer, but when it is, it's the *only* answer." With that in mind, let's move on. As we do so, I'd like to suggest that you try to look at the human body in purely physical terms—think of it as a "thing" that can be broken, like a piece of wood. Doing so really helps to reduce the emotional tenor that most of us apply to this topic.

VIOLENCE IS ALL ABOUT INJURY

All acts of violence come down to the same thing: injury. Until you accept this fundamental reality, you'll never be able to defend yourself effectively.

In a violent conflict, *always* assume that your life is at stake. Although you can predict how your attacker will react physically to being struck, how he reacts psychologically will vary from individual to individual. Some people may panic and run; others may be even more enraged that you dared to oppose them. Therefore, you must be focused and methodical. Once he's down, you may kick the head, stomp on the ankle, or drop your knee onto the crotch.

If someone is determined to kill you, you must place injury to ensure he can no longer hurt you. If he is still able to come after you, you must assume he will. Hopefully you're wrong, but if you're not, you don't want to leave your family to mourn your mistake.

Violence has no place in everyday life. If you're sane and socialized, then you probably can't imagine committing an injury on someone—that's a good thing. This book is not about becoming a violent person; it is about placing injury on a person who is trying to attack you so that you may survive.

Therefore, I say emphatically again that violence is a last resort. It's a very narrow tool good for only one thing, and that's shutting down a human being who intends to attack you. But if you are going to place an injury, then you must be prepared to employ it full force. When violence is necessary, every technique and every target must be utilized, even those you normally might regard as out of bounds. If, for example, you are afraid to go for someone's eye, but the only target available to you is his eye, your hesitation might very well cost you your life.

Level the Playing Field

Superior physical ability, knowledge, and experience, even an iron will, are all trumped by a thumb in the eye. There is nothing anyone can do to make themselves immune to the laws of the physical universe. Bullets are not swayed by bravado or presence; they are maddeningly impartial. Anyone can be violent, and no one is immune to violence.

These two facts are simultaneously reassuring and terrifying: You can apply it to anyone, but anyone can also apply it to you. We tell ourselves comforting lies to deal with it ("If I do this or that, there's nothing he can do to overwhelm me," and "If I'm stronger/faster/meaner, I'll be better off"), but you're much better off accepting the reality of it: All you can ever really do is level the playing field.

Knowing how to use violence as a survival tool—and being willing to do so—puts you on even, flat terrain, even and equal with the worst of humanity. You can see predators who stalk among us taking advantage of others' weakness. Before you learned how to grab the tool of violence in both fists and swing it hard, you were at a disadvantage. Now that disadvantage is gone. You have a choice: You can be afraid, or you can be committed.

THE INJURY MANIFESTO

There is a single key in every successful application of violence: injury. It defines the act and brands the participants, the vanquished more so than the victor. Owning and understanding injury, the arbiter of success in violence, gives you a distinct advantage.

Violence begins and ends with injury. It is the only thing that matters in a physically violent conflict. It defines the violent act and finishes it. The hallmark of effective violence in self-protection is serial injury: targeting properly and injuring him, taking advantage of that injury to do it again, and then repeating to make absolutely certain he is unable to get up and come after you.

Injury changes everything in your favor. In a violent conflict, injury is the portal through which you pass into the rest of your life. As things go bad—he pulls the gun—your options narrow to a single question: action or passivity? In a way, you are at the end of your life: If he shoots you dead, it's over. Getting your thumb in his eye, however, turns the key in the lock on the rest of your days. Injury gives you options instead of being paralyzed by fear. Injury creates the opportunity to escape a deadly attack.

Injury is objective. Even disinterested third parties can all agree that an injury has occurred. A broken leg is obvious from across the street.

Injury significantly impairs bodily function. It alters the normal functioning of his body in a negative way. A broken leg can't be walked on. A ruptured eyeball can no longer see. A smashed hand can no longer hold a knife.

Injury is permanent. That is, it impairs the attacker throughout the encounter. And it requires medical attention to heal. A broken leg does not get better on its own. He can't "walk it off." In other words, we're not talking about an owie.

Injury is where physics and physiology meet—badly. Injury is what happens when excessive force meets a vulnerable

VIOLENCE IS A LAST RESORT

Using violence to solve social problems is like using a crowbar to open your car door: It'll do the job, but it'll cause a whole heap of other problems. Violence is the last resort, when communication isn't an option and it's injure or be injured. Violence is what you use the moment you feel threatened.

If you realize it's possible to talk your way out of a difficult situation, doing that should be your first choice. Often, an aggressive person will put on a show to try to dominate you without actually resorting to violence. They'll make themselves look bigger, scream obscenities, or issue threats. Sometimes, they're just trying to intimidate you in the hope that you'll back down. Sometimes, they're psyching themselves up for violence. You

SURVIVE THE UNTHINKABLE

anatomical target. There's nothing in this equation about pain or the psychological state of the recipient. Neither of these matters. Different people have different pain thresholds; a torn fingernail drops some people into dramatic paroxysms of agony, but others won't notice a torn-off limb, at least temporarily. But note that although the latter person may be functioning just fine psychologically, they're not going to be using that limb anytime soon.

have to decide which it is and act accordingly if you feel there's a real threat. Once you decide to act, act immediately and decisively.

If you don't believe a problem can be resolved with language and diplomacy, say nothing. Don't look the person in the eye or engage in conversation. When you enter into a conversation with a threatening or asocial person, you enter a gray zone in which it's much harder to disengage and strike the first blow. Leave if you can. Again, violence isn't always the answer, but when it is the answer, it's the only answer.

Use violence only when you have no other choice.
And once you start, you're not done until you finish it on *your* terms.

Injury is independent of technique. All you need is force and a target. You could trip and fall all by yourself and get injured—without being in a hopped-up emotional state, using a technique, or even involving another person. This fact is why technique without injury is only a parlor trick, and injury, regardless of how it occurred (with technique or by accident) will always be more effective. The most artless injury inflicted will always be superior to the fanciest technique used without injuring. You don't need to learn jiu-jitsu to protect yourself.

All injuries are equal. This is another way of saying that all targets are equal. The best target? The one you just wrecked. All injuries are equal when you know what to do next to take advantage of the fact that you injured the person.

Injured people move in predictable ways. The body responds to injury through the somatic reflex arc (the reflexes processed solely by the spinal cord). These are specific automatic movements triggered by large stimuli (like ruptured testicles). The threshold switch that decides whether or not to reflex is in the spinal cord, not the brain. There is no conscious choice involved, just physics and physiology. These reflexes are injury specific, meaning that a boot to the groin elicits the same basic response in all humans. This means you can predict how he'll move when you injure him—and be there to take full advantage of it (we'll discuss this further).

Injured people are helpless. For the short time they are in the throes of their spinal reflex, they cannot stop you from injuring them again and getting away.

Injury begets injury. Because injured people are helpless, beating an injured man is easy work. In this way, then, a broken knee can cause other trauma when the injured person topples to the ground.

Injury trumps strength, speed, and resolve. Is he stronger than you? Not if you have knocked the wind out of him. Is he faster than you? Not with a damaged knee. Is he far more dangerous than you, with scads of training, experience, a gun, and an indomitable iron will? Not if you have successfully targeted and struck him so he is incapacitated from hurting you again.

Anything you do in a violent situation that does not cause an injury is worthless to you. Every time you touch him, you need to interrupt normal functioning. Every time you touch him, you need to make a part of him cease normal functioning. You're not done until you're sure he's not able to come after you.

The answer to every question in a violent conflict is: Injure him, right now.

WHAT IS INJURY, REALLY?

Injury is the most important part of violence, and it's an enormous part of your education. But what is injury, really? And is there a simpler way to think of it, relate to it, and thereby better relate it to others? We'll start with the standard definition of the word:

*Hurt or loss caused to or sustained by
a person or thing; harm, detriment;
damage, esp. to the body; an instance of this.*

—THE SHORTER OXFORD
ENGLISH DICTIONARY, 5TH EDITION

This is a great start, but it's not quite as serious and stunning as I would like. While "harm," "detriment," and "damage" are all good synonyms for what I'm advocating, it's still a bit vague on the overall effect I'm gunning for. There are plenty of people out there, for example, who believe that they can sustain "damage" and keep going. And, of course, they're right. We all can. But no one—*no one*—can sustain injury the way I mean it and keep going. Period. So even the dictionary definition leaves something to be desired, a "tightening up" of ambiguities.

No two people's definitions of "injury" are exactly the same. For some it is tearing a fingernail or stubbing a toe; others won't declare it accomplished until blood is spilled. The difference between the definitions given by a sheltered person and a trauma surgeon is vast. It's a lot like saying the word "dog" to a roomful of people: Everyone will see a dog in their mind's eye, but no two will be alike.

And still, for me, even with "torn skin" and "spilled blood," we are not at a workable definition. This is the definition I teach my students:

The disruption of human tissue in a specific anatomical feature such that its normal function is obviously impaired (and can only be regained through medical intervention) and an involuntary spinal reflex reaction is elicited.

This definition is useful for two reasons: It reinforces that there is a wide spectrum of violence (which can be inflicted with any sufficient application of any source of kinetic energy, from fist to stick to bullet), and it's also specific enough to rule out hangnails and messy but ultimately ineffective minor lacerations.

The only problem is that for all its precision, it's quite a mouthful and mind-full. It's thorough but clunky. Therefore, I offer my current favorite way to think of causing injury:

Break things about the person so they
don't work and can't harm you.

This is the way the sociopath approaches you, ready to deliver a beating. It is the simplest way to think of injury. It paints a picture that's easy to parse; even the ambiguities work in your favor. Does "they" refer to the person or the things inside them? Hey, either one or both: I'm good with all of it.

This is a definition of "injury" you can adopt as your violence mission statement. It's the only measuring stick that divides success from failure. Easy to think, easy to say, easy to do.

INJURY: A TOOL FOR SURVIVAL

In the end, you don't "win" in a violent conflict—you survive. It's not a competition, it's not a "fight," it's destruction. The survivor gets to walk away. The other guy doesn't. And far more often than not, the one who's walking away is the one who was being violent first.

It's only going to work out in your favor if you get in there and injure him first. You have to put him down and keep him there. You have to combine instinct with intellect. In deadly situations survival is the only thing that matters, and the best way to survive violence is to injure your attacker.

When you harm a target and make him react, you will have the time and the opportunity to injure him again and again and again. You will be in control of the situation, and of the other person. In other words, do unto others *before* they do unto you.

All of this flies in the face of what we consider a "fair" fight. But survival situations aren't fair fights. In a competitive fair fight, it's all about skill and ability. A violent situation is about survival: You must injure your attacker as fast and as much as you can, in any way possible. It's not something to be used lightly, but when it's the only alternative, it can save your life.

You have to put aside the social constraints and emotional shackles that make violence seem unimaginable. It's time to accept that, while social constraints are appropriate in 99 percent of everyday situations, you may one day find yourself facing a situation where they don't apply. And in that situation, you have to be able to slip them off and protect your own life.

CHAPTER SIX

YOUR ATTACKER IS MORE VULNERABLE THAN YOU THINK

Violence may cause injury, but targeting is what makes a successful injury—and, possibly, your survival. Poke your finger in someone's eye and he instantly collapses in agony. Miss by an inch, and you've just pissed him off. Even if you do all else perfectly, if you miss the target, even by a little, it will all be for nothing.

P. Michael Murphy, the Nevada county coroner I mentioned in Chapter Four, told me that many female victims have their attacker's skin under their fingernails, which means they put up a fight. Had they only poked those fingers into their attacker's eye, they might very well have survived.

WHAT FIGHTERS KNOW

The use of force leads to injury only when that force is applied to specific spots on the human body. This concept seems obvious, but all too often it gets lost in the actual application. If you've never done so (or even if you have), it's worthwhile to watch an MMA (mixed martial arts) competition for a very specific reason: As violent as these competitions appear to be, these athletes have an amazing ability to absorb what seems like relentless punishment during round after round, often with little or no apparent effect. Crushing kicks to the legs, sledgehammer blows to the body, and even ferocious knees to the face more times than not have very little obvious effect. You may wonder how these fighters can tolerate such blows. Is it because they have hardened their bodies through training, or maybe because they're simply a different type of human being?

Neither is true! There are two reasons that MMA athletes can withstand punishing blows like the ones I've just described:

1. Due to the chaos of the fight, most blows do not actually hit their intended targets.

2. As violent as MMA competitions seem, they're really not violent at all: Hitting the most vulnerable targets—the ones you'll need to find if your life is ever on the line—is not allowed in MMA.

Believe it or not, in the Ultimate Fighting Championship (perhaps the most popular form of MMA competition today) there are thirty-one fouls, which turn out to provide an excellent guide to what you *should* do in a dangerous or potentially fatal situation! There are a few exceptions (a few are iffy, and two are flat-out wrong), but in general, to survive a violent situation, you need to sometimes use counterintuitive measures.

Now, before you cringe over the following no-holds-barred list, remember that we are talking here about a life-or-death situation, one from which all other options for action have been removed. At that point, your goal is survival, and you'll do whatever it takes to live. Right?

Of the thirty-one MMA fouls, these are the ones that stand out as a blueprint for what to do—and what not to do—in a violent conflict.

Yes

Gouging the eyes. Eyes are one of the three targets that do not require the force of your body weight to injure. Don't avoid this target because some silly "rule" says to or you feel squeamish about it.

Attacking the groin. This is the second of the three targets that do not require the force of your body weight.

Striking the throat. Grabbing the trachea (the windpipe) is one example of a throat strike. Again, you don't need your body weight behind a move to cause a serious injury here.

Pulling the hair. If your attacker has long enough hair, you can use it as a handle to perform a more intense strike.

Putting a finger into any orifice, cut, or laceration. Doing only this may just cause discomfort, but if you roll him over using his broken elbow, for example, then I'm all for it.

Manipulating small joints. This is code for "breaking fingers."

Striking the spine or the back of the head. This is going for the central nervous system. Serious, lifelong disability or death can result from head or spine trauma, so be careful here. This obviously is unacceptable in a sports competition, but it could mean the difference between life and death in a deadly, violent conflict.

Striking downward using the point of the elbow. Here, you use gravity to deliver a blow that carries the force of your body weight, which can be more effective than a punch. The point of the elbow is the smallest, hardest striking surface on your body. Line it up with a target like the spine or neck and you have a good shot at ending the fight.

Clawing, pinching, or twisting the flesh. As an isolated act, this is simply painful. As an adjunct to something vicious (like a throw or a joint break), it's a powerful and effective move. Think of the human body as a jumpsuit with handles all over it and grab whatever you need to and use it to your advantage.

Grabbing the clavicle (collarbone). By itself, this is merely painful. It becomes useful, however, if you think of the clavicle as a handle, which you can use to force someone to the ground.

Kicking or kneeing the head of a grounded opponent.

Stomping on a grounded opponent. Driving your body weight downward through your leg and foot may result in a fight-ending injury.

Throwing an opponent out of the ring or fenced area. In our context, this means throwing someone into something that will cause injury, like a fire hydrant or a plate-glass window.

Holding the clothing of an opponent. Although doing this is useless as an isolated move, doing it to help you throw your attacker is brilliant.

Attacking an opponent unexpectedly. Attacking when he's not expecting it will work to your advantage.

Maybe

Head butting. Can it work? Sure. Is it a good idea? Hardly. You don't want to come into that close contact with your attacker.

Biting. Like head butting, this can work, but you should figure out a better alternative.

"Fish hooking," or inserting your fingers into someone's mouth and pulling or ripping the mouth apart from the sides. This can work if it is your only option, but you run the risk of getting your fingers chewed on.

No Way

Spitting. This probably won't deter him. If you're throwing sand or a liquid into your attacker's eyes in order to blind him, then it may be effective. Still, don't be afraid to use your own body to inflict injury.

Using abusive language. Once you've crossed over into violence, threats and slurs will get you nowhere. There should be no communication once the fighting has begun.

Throwing in the towel. In real life, if you quit, you die. End of story.

The point is, real violence isn't a game. Real violence breaks all the rules. That means you'd better be ready to break them, too.

TARGETS—WHERE INJURIES WORK

You can punch a man in the forehead as hard as you want, but all you're going to get is a broken hand. If you break his nose instead, you're off to a much better start.

This is because some parts of the human body are tougher and less susceptible to harm than others. In general, you want to strike the parts of the body that are predisposed to injury.

The points on the human body that are effective targets correspond to three important criteria:

1. They are the places where injuries typically occur.

2. They're important to normal, effective functioning.

3. They have specific associated spinal reflexes (the "cause" and "effect" states that we'll discuss in the next chapter).

These are not pressure points or mystical "energy lines" or anything remotely similar. They have technical, anatomical names, but you can call them anything you want as long as you know where they are. These are the places where most sports injuries tend to occur, so watching sports is an effective way to study self-protection targets: Just turn on a football game. These are the places on the human body that get wrecked when people crash into each other or get knocked to the ground. And that's exactly what you need to know in order to protect yourself.

The targets are critical body parts or access points to body systems that your attacker needs to sense the world around him, to breathe, to think, and to move. When these targets are damaged, he won't be so good at doing those things anymore. Most important, he won't be able to come after you.

For example, a blow to the solar plexus—a bundle of nerves behind the stomach—will interrupt normal breathing. A broken kneecap will prevent him from coming after you. Seriously injuring any one of these targets kicks off a spinal reflex that will force him to move in a predictable fashion, stopping him in his tracks and giving you the opportunity to escape.

Outward Focus

Before you can even think about hitting a target, you must first replace fear with what I call "outward focus." The moment you become aware that you might be in danger, your mind will automatically ask, "Oh, no, what's he going to do to me?" This type of inward focus is very natural, very understandable, and also very dangerous. That's because you can't focus on how you're going to injure *him* if you're already worried about how he's going to injure *you*—and it's one or the other.

In any violent encounter, the survivor will be the person with the greatest degree of outward focus, or single-minded purpose. If you focus on injuring a man by striking vulnerable targets on his body, you have a chance of surviving the encounter. If you instead focus on what might happen to you, you have little chance of surviving. The choice is yours—and although that choice isn't easy, it is indeed simple.

Remember: *Nothing* happens if you "sort of" hit the target. You have to hit the target dead-on and with enough body weight behind it to wreck it.

This is why it's doubly important not just to study the target list, but also to slowly and methodically practice surgically precise targeting on a real human being. As you practice, so will you perform; if you don't practice hitting targets, you won't hit them when your life depends on it.

IT'S NOT ABOUT FITNESS, IT'S ABOUT ACCURACY

Some people who come to me seem to be looking for an exercise program, not techniques for self-protection. Over and over, I get confused looks and comments like "Okay, I'll do that, but what type of workout should I do?" They want me to give them a strength-training workout to improve their power and (even though most won't admit it) their body composition.

No matter how fit or strong you are, the best way to hone your self-protection skills is to focus on targeting. After that, you can certainly improve your physical fitness to increase the level of intensity you deliver to those targets.

I tell people over and over that the best way to hit "harder" is to focus on hitting your targets. No amount of strength or physical fitness can replace accuracy. I encourage people to practice a simple drill: Throughout the day, constantly look for targets on the people you see in the streets, at the mall or grocery store, and so on. The best way to improve a skill is to constantly practice it in nonstressful settings. Then, if you ever encounter a stressful situation, your brain will naturally seek out this familiar skill set. Visualization is a method commonly used by professional athletes in order to practice their focus and enhance their confidence—the more they can see themselves making an important play or scoring a goal, the better their actual performance during game time.

If you want an exercise program, by all means, go to the gym. I think it's a great idea to get and stay in shape, and I encourage everyone to maintain their physical fitness. But that issue is completely different from using violence as a tool. Your physical fitness level counts for nothing in a fight compared with your ability to hit a target. Targeting is what may save your life.

CHAPTER SEVEN

CAUSE AND EFFECT

Isaac Newton told us that in nature, every action produces an equal and opposite reaction. The same is true of violence: A specific injury will cause a specific, involuntary defensive movement.

For example, you know that if you accidentally touch a hot surface, your hand instantly flies away from the heat source without your even making a conscious decision to do so. By the time the pain stimulus travels from your hand to your head, you've already pulled your hand away. If the neural impulse had to travel all the way to your brain and prompt you to make a decision before you could act, you'd be pulling back a lump of charcoal. Pulling your hand away from something that's very hot is a physiological reflex based in the spine that separates you from danger as quickly as possible. There's no decision process involved and no way to stop the reaction.

Heat isn't the only source of unstoppable reactions in people. Other kinds of injury often have similar predictable effects. Recall for a moment that your primary goal in any violent conflict is to injure your attacker so he reacts involuntarily. When you do this correctly, you control the situation.

Whoever causes the first effect—makes the other person react first—stands the greatest chance of winning. That doesn't mean that you will always win if you land the initial blow. Nor does it mean you will inevitably lose if he strikes first. It usually takes more than one effect to shut a person down; you win when you cause a *series of effects* that leads to his incapacitation. If you hesitate to accept an opportunity created by an effect or fail to make use of your own action (or reaction), you'll lose.

THE CAUSE STATE

When you understand the nature of cause and effect in violence, you'll be able to use that knowledge to overpower your attacker or recover from a blow.

The person in the Cause State is the one who makes things happen. In violence, that's the person inflicting injury upon the other.

I know this sounds crazy, but you *need* to be that person. You need to be that person because the alternative is not survivable. The alternative is this: *You're* down and getting stomped, *you're* getting stabbed, *you're* getting shot.

You want to be the one *causing* the effects, not the other way around. You want to be the one injuring another—in order to protect yourself. There are two things you'll need to make this happen. You need to have intent, and you need to know how to target effectively.

Intent: Injury isn't going to happen all by itself. It's not going to happen unless you throw your entire being into the process of getting it done. You're going to dish out serious injury only if serious injury is your goal. If you hang back because you're afraid he'll counter you, then guess what—that's exactly what will happen. You'll do nothing more than piss him off. But if you go in with *intent*, you'll snap his ribs and bruise his liver. You'll knock the wind right out of him and escape without further injury yourself. But you have to want it, because injury doesn't happen without intent.

It's important to note that intent has nothing to do with a heightened emotional state. It's not about being enraged, pumped up, or scared. You don't have to whip yourself into a frenzy or "unleash the animal within." Intent is simply the single-minded desire to survive, to the exclusion of all else. It's the answer to the question "Do you want to survive this violent conflict?" When you say yes, what you really mean is that you want to injure your attacker. If you want to injure him, then get in there and do it like you mean it. Think about this for a minute, and then reread this paragraph. Are you with me? Having this mind-set is how you survive.

Targeting: As we discussed in the previous chapter, good targeting pays off, regardless of his size or strength. If you don't hit a target, you won't seriously injure the person, no matter how hard you hit, no matter how much intent you have. He'll just keep right on coming.

It's not enough to *want* to hurt someone—you have to

strike the precise point on the human body that is susceptible to that injury. A fist to the forehead may result in nothing more than a broken hand. But a finger in the eye likely rewards you with the rest of your life. The difference between the two is difficult to overstate; in one, you probably injured yourself and gave him the upper hand; in the other, you blinded him and gave yourself the time and opportunity to break his knee. And yet the difference is really very small, isn't it? There's only an inch or two between the eye and the forehead. But what a critical amount it is!

This is why my system is called Target Focus Training. If you focus on your targets, if you build the skill of being able to strike with precision, you will be the dominant force in any violent encounter. You'll most likely get to walk away and enjoy the rest of your life.

NEVER, EVER HESITATE

The principles of the Cause State are very simple: Injure your attacker. Strike *now*. Continue causing injury until you're satisfied that he is no longer a threat. The only safe action to take in a violent encounter is to cause an effect. As long as you are striking your opponent, you're on the offensive and you have control—unless you make a mistake.

That mistake is typically some form of hesitation. Missing a target, pausing to see how things are going, lacking the will to kick a man when he's down, jumping around in a fighting stance. All these things are opportunities for him to recover from your last shot and hurt you. This is why you must never give him the opportunity to recover and continue to attack you. You have to control the situation from the moment you cause the first injury. And you will survive when you use that control to break him down.

The reverse is true as well—if your attacker hesitates or makes a mistake, it gives you a critical advantage that you must use to survive. For example, say you are attacked in an empty parking lot. The guy lunges at you and starts hitting you with his fists. You may put up your arms to ward off the blow, but this only results in broken fingers. The second shot breaks your arm. The third shot connects with your head, and you go down. And then it's just more of the same, with his arm rising and falling repeatedly, pulping your head.

You have two options for making it out alive: hope he stops or misses, or decide to injure him—*now*.

If he hesitates or misses, you have an opportunity to get in there and injure him. Backing up or attempting to counter his "technique" with another technique (as is typically taught in self-defense classes) will only get you in more trouble. For one, the human body is a lot better at going forward than it is at going backward, and for every two feet you can move backward, he can move forward three feet.

The other problem with countering your attacker's blows is that it requires you to wait and see what's coming and then try to do something about it. This works fine when everybody agrees that it does, like in a staid and cooperative martial arts class, but in that parking lot, he's probably not going to play along. Stage magicians say that the hand is quicker than the eye, and the business end of his fist will be even faster than that. This means that you're a half step behind him, and instead of countering, or even catching up, all you're going to do is catch the edge of his knuckles.

If, on the other hand, you summon your will—*"I want to survive"*—and move straight to the offensive, you can injure him at the first opportunity. Maybe you'll lunge forward and punch him in the throat as he cocks his arm. You'll then press your advantage by kicking him in the kneecap as he staggers back, choking. You've taken control of the situation by forcing him to react to what *you* are doing. You won't stop—just like he wouldn't have—until he's down and not getting back up.

DECISIVE ACTION IN THE FACE OF FEAR

Eddie Rickenbacker, a top American fighter pilot in World War I, said, "There can be no courage unless you're scared." He was, of course, absolutely right: The first effect in any violent situation is the experience of emotion, and the most common emotion in this case is fear. When a man steps out of the shadows holding a knife or an intruder pulls open the curtain in your shower, your adrenaline immediately starts pumping and your heart beats faster. These are natural reactions that cannot be avoided—nor should they be. This is the fight-or-flight survival instinct that allows you to focus completely on destroying your enemy or to get the hell out of there.

Many people fear that they will be overwhelmed by fight-or-flight and behave irrationally or "freeze up" and be incapable of acting.

When you know how to "swim in the pool of violence," however, your reaction will be slightly different. You will still feel a certain amount of fear that you could be hurt, or that you're about to cause harm to another human being, but that will be tempered with confidence. Instead of being shocked and frightened and believing you have no choice but to submit, you'll realize that the confidence of the man is misplaced. He believes his weapon or his strength is enough to give him victory; you know that the most powerful weapon in violence is control, and you know how to take it from him—by injuring him.

You perform as you train: The first thing that happens in a violent situation tends to be the thing you trained yourself to do. If you're trained to hesitate or to get in a ready stance, then you're going to be stuck doing that. If you're trained to step in and strike at the first sign of a threat, that's what you'll do.

Being trained in the effective use of violence as a survival tool will diminish the chaos of the situation, and the fear of the unknown. When you know what to do, how to do it, and what the result will be, you are more likely to act with confidence, even in the face of fear.

The people I have trained who later had to use their skills in real violent conflicts typically reported that the situation was over before they really had time to think about being afraid or worry about how it was all going to work out. They simply stepped in and got the job done. Every single one of them experienced the physiological symptoms of fear—the fight-or-flight reflex—but none of them were overwhelmed by it. They were too busy doing other things, like causing injury.

A STATE OF CONSTANT ATTACK

In violent conflict, if you're not injuring someone, then you're getting injured. When you're on the defensive—trying to block, backing off instead of charging forward, or begging him to stop as the blows are raining down—it's only a matter of time before you'll get walloped with a killer punch. Look at it this way: Instead of worrying about what he's doing, make him worry about what *you're* doing.

These principles are *not* a defensive "fighting" technique or a modern martial art. They're simply a methodical way to use violence to injure people and end the situation in your favor. To do this, you need to keep in mind that no matter what the circumstances, there is always a way to injure him. You just have to find it. Thinking otherwise is giving up and potentially assisting in your own demise.

If you follow the methods and principles taught in this book, you'll come out on top, but you won't necessarily do it without a scratch. To think that you can make it through a violent assault without injury is dangerously naïve, and I'd be doing you a grave disservice if I told you anything else. In real violence you're going to get hit. If there's a knife, you're going to get cut. If there's a stick, you're going to get smacked with it. The gun always goes off. These are constants that you can bank on.

Clearly, nobody wants any of these things to happen, but if you go in with that fear—"I don't want to get cut"—then you'll freak out when it does happen. If you go in supremely dedicated to surviving, supremely dedicated to injuring him, no matter what, then you will. You may be bloodied, bruised, and walking away with a limp, but he won't be walking away at all.

Again: The best way to survive a violent conflict is to be the first one to cause an injury. When you destroy a target and make him react, you will have the time and the opportunity to injure him again and again—and walk away with your life.

FROM INJURED TO NONFUNCTIONAL

In a violent conflict, you want to injure him first and then continue injuring him until he's nonfunctional and no longer a threat. This means different things to different people based on their experience, what it takes for them to feel safe, and the circumstances surrounding the situation.

If it's clear that the situation is life or death, then you must make a choice about who is to be killed: you or your attacker. Too many domestic violence stories include a woman confessing, "I think he's going to kill me," and then days later, he does. Your survival is ultimately your decision. And your best guideline, believe it or not, is to trust your gut. If you don't feel it's a particularly bad situation, you're probably picking up unconscious cues from his body language or facial expressions that are telling you he's not serious. If you feel serious apprehension in your gut—that queasy "oh my god" feeling—you're picking up unconscious cues, but this time they warn of lethal intent. He means to kill you, and primitive parts of your brain are trying to let you know by making you feel sick.

I can't list every possible scenario you could ever be involved in, and I can't tell you how you should think and feel. But I can give you the tools to survive if that's your choice.

If you decide to survive a life-or-death attack, you'll need to render him nonfunctional. How far you take it will depend on what you need to feel safe enough to be able to turn your back on him and walk away. This can mean one or more of three things:

Incapacitation. This is everything from a single blow to the ribs that drops him into a fetal position and makes him quit to a broken knee and two broken collarbones that make it impossible for him to get up. At what point you've reached incapacitation and can stop is your personal judgment call. Just make damn sure you feel comfortable turning your back on him.

Unconsciousness. He's out cold and down for the count. It's obvious when you've achieved it. He'll be down, motionless, possibly with his jaw slack and his eyes rolled back in his head. Once you've got this, it's safe to say you're done.

Death. Killing the man by stomping on his throat, breaking his neck, or stabbing him in the heart. This level of violence must be reserved for the most extreme circumstances only—situations in which you realize or believe that you or others will be killed if you do not act. You need to think a great deal about how you feel about this and make your choices ahead of time—you don't want to get caught hesitating when what's required is decisive action.

When faced with violent conflict, you must keep a single goal in mind: injuring your attacker. You don't have time to think about defending yourself or others, or saving your property or honor. Protecting those things is a side effect of what you're engaged in, and you'll be the winner only after the fact. In the actual moment of violence, your intent must be solely to cause injury in order to survive.

You can be sure the criminal sociopath coming after you isn't distracted. He's not worried about the contents of his wallet, "defending" himself, or even getting back home tonight. He's 100 percent focused on taking you out. To have any hope of taking him out instead, you have to go in with that same singular focus. Everything you do must cause injury, for no other reason than to get it done.

THE EFFECT STATE

Compared with the Cause State, the Effect State is very simple. Whereas the Cause State requires instruction and knowledge, the Effect State is a single physiological fact: *Living things move away from negative stimuli.*

Or, more simply put, if you poke a cat with a sharp stick, it'll run away.

It's important to note that the cat won't push itself against the stick—it will go the other direction, in much the same way that if you strike a man in the throat, he will move backward,

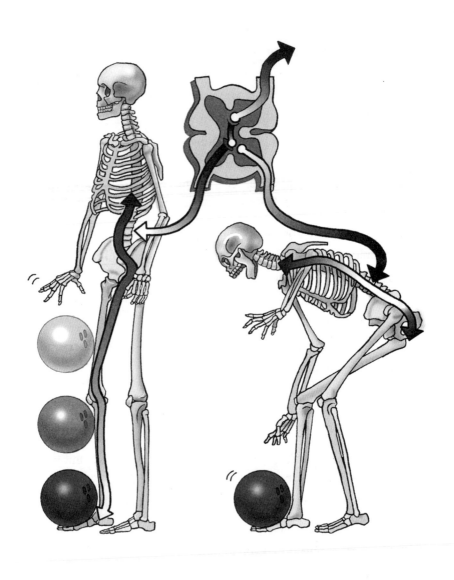

The Effect State—when an attacker is vulnerable

SURVIVE THE UNTHINKABLE

away from the strike. The man won't hold still, and he won't keep coming at you. He's going to move away to get his crushed throat off your fist.

When the negative stimulus is a truly debilitating injury (like a crushed throat), the reaction to move away is dramatic, involuntary, and specific. This is because the body's response to injury is a *spinal reflex*. A spinal reflex is a specific involuntary preprogrammed movement that occurs in response to an injury, mediated by a threshold switch in the top of the spinal cord. It does not involve the brain per se, or even conscious thought. If you kick a man in the groin, rupturing one or both testicles, he will bend his knees, put his hands over his groin, and bend forward at the hips with his chin up, every single time—*even if he doesn't want to.*

The image on the opposite page illustrates the Effect State. As soon as the bowling ball hits the foot, a signal races through nerves toward the brain to let the person know he's been injured. As the signal fires along the spinal cord, it hits a threshold switch near the top of the spine. This switch is tripped if the signal is strong enough. If the signal is mild, like from a slightly stubbed toe, the switch may not be tripped, and instead the signal continues on to the brain, where it registers the fact that this injury happened, as well as the minor discomfort being felt.

In this case, the signal is coming from a crushed foot—a serious injury—triggering a cascade of events. Motor impulses are sent to the legs to shift balance and move the body away from the ball. The arms flare to keep the body balanced, then retract to cover the site of the injury and prevent further harm.

Depending on the specific injury, motor impulses may also be sent to turn or drop the head so the person can see what's going on at the site of the injury. All this movement is involuntary—the person doesn't get to decide whether or not to do it. It is a hardwired reflex that takes place in the spine, not the brain. After the reflex has jerked the body into a protective posture, the person will *then* feel any pain caused by the injury and realize that something has happened. It's extremely important to note that all this motion happens before there is any sensation of pain or even the conscious realization of what has occurred.

IT'S NOT ABOUT PAIN

The subjective perception of pain has nothing to do with spinal reflexes. This is a fancy way of saying, "It doesn't matter how bad it hurts, only how broken it is."

Some people have very high pain tolerance. People who are in an altered state (such as in shock, furious, drunk, or drugged) may feel no pain at all. Pain and how it affects different people at different times is a psychological variable. This means that sometimes it works, and sometimes it doesn't. In order to be 100 percent effective, we have to discard the notion of pain as a useful tool in violence.

It is not pain that causes the spinal reflex—it's the injury that does it. You don't want to "hurt" him; you need to injure him.

How Targeted Injuries Work to Your Advantage

Each target on the human body gives rise to a specific and unique reaction when injured. There are, however, several elements common to all reactions:

◇ The head and hands move toward the injury.

◇ The body rotates in the direction of a strike.

◇ Strikes above the solar plexus (which is just below the sternum, or breastbone) bend the body backward; strikes below the solar plexus bend it forward. When a person is in the throes of a spinal reflex, he is helpless. He literally can do nothing but react. This gives you an opportunity to injure him again—but only if you stay right on top of him. He won't be stuck reacting forever; most reactions are over and done with in a split second. Recovering from a reaction and regaining balance and control over the body take mere seconds. This is a critical time frame in which you must injure him again, before he can recover. This doesn't mean you need to go fast. It means you have to be efficient. You need to injure him, then injure him again, and so on in a calculated, methodical fashion.

The ultimate goal is to injure him, dropping him into the Effect State, and then keep him there, helpless to stop you, until you've finished. Each injury gives you the opportunity to injure him again. You need to use that to grind him through a steady downward spiral from the initial injury into a sustained

Effect State with serial injuries or, if necessary, render him nonfunctional.

Here's an example of how effective, targeted striking can capitalize on cause and effect to enable you to survive a potentially deadly situation.

A man approaches you as you're fumbling for your keys in front of your apartment building, and he pulls a knife on you about to attack you. You immediately claw him in the face, targeting his eyes with your fingers. His head snaps back and his hands fly up to his face, covering it, as he steps back away from you.

While he's busy doing this, you kick him in the groin as hard as you can. He jerks forward, bending over and reaching for his groin.

Now you strike him in the back of the neck as hard as you can with your elbow. He pitches forward onto the ground. You kick him in the ribs as hard as you can.

At this point you notice that he's not really moving. He's been immobilized, and that means you can walk away. You feel safe enough to turn your back and quickly unlock your front door and step inside, locking it behind you.

This scenario is the ideal expression of what I'm talking about. It's serial injury without pause, a rhythmic cascade of harm delivered relentlessly from start to finish. When it's done right, there's nothing the man can do to save himself.

Once he's injured, if you miss your target or let him get away from you, rest assured that he'll be coming right back at you, but with one important deficit: Some part of him won't be working anymore. If you were able to injure him and get a spinal reflex in the first place, then you broke something in him, and all is not lost. Get in there and break something else to put him back in the Effect State. Then keep it up, giving him injury after injury to keep him there until you're done.

HOW TO KNOW YOU ARE CAUSING INJURY

Violent encounters can be chaotic, fast, and scary. How do you know if what you're doing is working to disable your opponent and allow you to escape? "Targeting" is the ultimate expression of your intent to end the conflict, and the easiest road to causing effects. Understanding where to injure someone not only offers the best shot at crippling your attacker, but also allows you to know, at every turn, how much trauma you've inflicted.

In other words, the feedback you get from causing injury (the severity or absence of a reaction) will tell you how injured he is and whether or not he's in the Effect State. If you kicked him in the groin and he's now doubled over in pain, you did it right, and you now have a chance to inflict another strike to knock him to the ground. If he's standing there catching his breath but not in severe pain, you know you didn't injure him and you need to get in there and do it again until you get it right.

Without understanding the relationship between targets and reactions, you might miss the signs of any injuries you have caused in the chaos of a violent encounter. Instead of aiming for specific parts of the body, your potential target will be lumped into one big mass—the entire human body—when actually, there are more than 70 different anatomic locations

Gaining Tactical Advantage

Knowing how your attacker will move when you injure him allows you to move him wherever and into whatever position you want. For example, imagine that you want to kick him in the head but you're unable to reach your target because he's taller than you. You could kick him in the knee to dislocate his kneecap, causing him to bend forward and bringing his head down to his hip level. You could then deliver a blow to his head, knocking him to the ground and possibly rendering him unconscious.

Let's say there are two attackers, and the one farther from you has a gun. When you injure the first man, you don't want to knock him away or down—you want to keep him up and in front of you to block the other guy's line of fire while you close the distance. You don't want to strike him in the throat, because that would make him move away

that can cause a spinal reflex when injured, and nearly 200 different targets to exploit them.

Because every target yields a slightly different reaction and each reaction is an indicator of the associated trauma to that target, you can see that targeting and the feedback generated by your strikes provide you with the measurements you need to be sure you are dropping your attacker into the Effect State.

For example, if you want to "knock the wind" out of a man, an obvious way to do that is by kicking him in the groin. You from you. If you did, you would have to grab the back of his neck to keep him from moving away as you strike his throat using your other arm, because you want to keep him upright and between you and the guy with the gun.

Or, conversely, let's say there's one guy between you and a door, and all you really want to do is get through that door as fast as you can. When you injure the man, you don't want him to be in front of you, getting in your way. So you should strike him in the side of his neck, injuring him and knocking him out of your way to the side so you are free to run out the door while he's busy reacting.

When you understand the specific reactions that occur with specific injuries, deriving answers to problems like these becomes easier. Knowing your options gives you a better chance of surviving in a critical moment.

can assess your progress by the reaction you see. If the man shifts a step to the side rather than bending straight over, that means you missed the groin and instead struck the saphenous nerve on the inner side of the thigh. You know the man still "has his wind" and that you need to use that reaction to give him another shot (hopefully one that achieves what you want it to). By using his reactions to measure your success, you're able to establish and stay on the offensive while subjecting him to further injury.

BIGGER, STRONGER, MEANER, AND ARMED

Imagine you're facing a man who is bigger than you, stronger than you—and, clearly, meaner than you. And he has a knife. How could you possibly overcome his superior size and strength? His cruel stare? And what's he going to do with that knife?

All those questions vanish once you launch the hard toe of your shoe into his groin—his size and strength become meaningless as he momentarily loses control over his body and executes a picture-perfect groin reaction. He's still mean—but he can't do anything with it. His will has been trumped by the threshold switch at the top of his spine.

And what's he doing with that knife? Nothing. He's still in the middle of reacting to a painful groin injury. Find your next target while he's busy, injure him again, and then repeat until you are sure he is unable to use that knife on you.

Injured people move in involuntary, predictable ways. Applying your target training to this fact can make the difference between your achieving calculated, methodical success and succumbing to utter chaos. You can struggle and hope things go your way, or you can injure him, drop him into the Effect State, and never let him go until you're done.

VIOLENCE AS A SURVIVAL TOOL

In the Cause State you are *causing* the violence. In the Effect State, he is *reacting* to the violence you have caused. He has *no freedom* to choose his actions. If he is injured in a particular way and in a particular place, he can do little more than watch his body move against his will. And when you know how his body will react, you'll have the ability to use that motion to your advantage.

There is nothing mystical, magical, or philosophical about these two states. One simply follows the other. You do not need to get worked up, go berserk, or be a devoted nihilist in order to injure someone. Likewise, there is no way for someone to harden himself or herself against the effects of serious injury. Stabbing someone in the eye requires only a small physical motion—and every human on the planet responds to the injury in the same hardwired, predictable way.

Cause and effect, and how they work in violence, are facts. Facts you can use to impose order on an otherwise chaotic and frightening scenario—smashing your way through violent conflict and coming out alive on the other side.

Uncomfortable as they may be, knowing these facts gives you *options*: You can either wield the tool of violence or feel its sting.

CHAPTER EIGHT

THE HUMAN MACHINE

When you think of a weapon, you might imagine anything from a spear or knife to a gun, or even a heat-seeking missile. That's a pretty wide range—what could a lowly club and a nuclear warhead possibly have in common?

Well, they were all developed by the human brain. Being stalked by bigger, stronger predators on the savanna was an incredible motivator for people. It likely contributed to our brains' evolution. Early humans were always on the lookout for an advantage, something to improve their odds, if only by a little bit. Hitting things with a heavy stick or rock was probably the first expression of that. In fact, you can think of those objects as the nuclear weapons of their day.

And much as we learned to use the stick, we developed nukes by looking at the natural world around us, figuring out how it worked, and then harnessing that power in a device for violence.

This makes the human brain one of the most dangerous things in the known universe.

This is a very important point, one that cannot be overstated: Your brain—*not your muscles*—is your most powerful asset in a violent conflict. Your brain is the ultimate weapon. Every solution you need for every violent situation will come from there. If we analyzed cases in which a woman either avoided or survived a violent attack perpetrated by a man (or men), we would likely see that the majority of the time, it was because she got lucky or because she used her brain.

Whatever the situation is, I encourage you to look at the cerebral option. Brainpower can be as subtle as listening to intuition as an early warning mechanism or putting the principles you're learning in this book into action: Act to injure him *now*, before he gets the chance to do it to you.

A UNIVERSAL WEAPON SYSTEM

The human body is an incredibly powerful and adaptable weapon system. The body can be used as a veritable battering ram, taking on all kinds of specialized postures to hammer away at problems requiring brute force to solve. It can also be braced and utilized as a catapult to hurl objects and a lever to pry them apart. This amazing tool is operated by one of the most dangerous objects in the universe: your brain.

We started out throwing rocks and sticks, and then found that hitting things with a rock lashed to the end of a stick worked what seemed like magic. We recognized the power of sharp edges and eventually developed the ax, the spear, the arrow, and ultimately the sword. Outfit a man with a bronze shield and a short sword, line him up in tight rows with a lot of other men, and pretty soon you have a giant, powerful army. But for all its size and might, that army's actions are controlled by human *minds*.

Never underestimate the power of the human mind—yours or his. For humans, there is truly no such thing as being unarmed.

This is why, in violent conflict, you have to get past the question of what he might be holding, or what he might be capable of doing. Separate his mind from his machine. Injury is the goal of violence, and breaking the connection between the brain and the body is the goal of injury. It doesn't matter which direction you go on this—breaking the body to deny the brain its primary tool or shutting off or limiting the power of the brain to make the tool inert. If he can think and move, he's dangerous. Take away either one (or both, for that matter), and he's no longer a threat.

THE TRIAD OF VIOLENCE

No matter who's doing it or under what circumstances, the successful use of violence is always the same. It's one person damaging another. It's cause and effect. But what happens when we look deeper? Are there any other similarities among violent acts? It turns out that there are. Immutable principles of physics and physiology underlie every successful use of violence.

There are three critical components that are not only present in every violent act, but also used exclusively by the party that is dominant at any particular point in time. In other words, every successful use of violence consists of these things:

⋄ Penetration

⋄ Rotation

⋄ Injury

How many ways are there to kick a man in the groin? There's really only one way—*as hard as you can*. You can be in front of him, off to his side, behind him, standing, sitting, on the floor, etc. Though there are thousands of "techniques" for getting it done, at its root the answer is always the same: *as hard as you can!*

Instead of technique, the effective use of violence is about understanding and employing the *principles* at work in every violent act. Effective violence starts with penetration, is driven home with rotation, and ends with injury.

Penetration

In order to injure someone with your bare hands, you need to be close enough to touch him. That's obvious, right? *Penetration* gets you to him so you can drive through him and beyond. It puts you on top of him, dominating his space, throwing him off balance, and maximizing the kinetic energy available for injury. This involves your body weight slamming into a single target. It's your elbow being driven through his ribs by the locomotive of your entire mass. It's stepping in to strike.

Penetration is the engine that drives all violence—your body weight in motion. Without it, you have no ability to cause injury. With it, you can destroy targets at will.

Using the Triad

Let's say you are accosted as you walk to your car in a dark parking lot. You turn around and suddenly are confronted by a large man with a leer on his face. You know he means to harm you, so it's time to act—*now*. You step in and punch the thug in the solar plexus, then grab his hand and break his wrist while slamming him down into the concrete.

Here's how you achieved penetration-rotation-injury:

1. You stepped in (penetrated into his space) and punched him (rotating your torso to throw the punch and follow all the way through) in the solar plexus, causing an injury to the target.

2. You then grabbed his hand (penetrated) and broke his wrist (rotated his hand with enough follow-through to cause the injury and take him to the ground), causing additional injuries.

Rotation

This is the follow-through. Rotation is how you take his balance and beat him down. It's the motion that carries you beyond the ribs you broke as you penetrated. It's rotating your entire musculature on the axis of your spine to drive your arm toward and completely through the target. It's the deep follow-through required to distort the rib cage enough to break it, just as it does when you hit a softball with a bat. Your power comes from rotating your hips to carry you *through* the object you're hitting.

Injury

This is the big one, the ultimate goal of violence. It's what you get when you penetrate to a target and rotate through it. Injuries don't happen on their own or because you wish they would. Causing serious, debilitating injury requires delivering a large wallop with a big slug of momentum for penetration and then driving it home and pushing all the way through the target with rotation. Good targeting skills, including a working knowledge of the targets that are especially prone to injury, are also critical.

Injury is the light at the end of the tunnel. It is the bright spot in the dark shroud of chaos that surrounds all violence. It is the way through, the way out, the way back home to your loved ones.

Effective use of violence always includes this triad—it powers everything from striking to joint breaking and throwing, even when you use tools like knives, sticks, sidewalk curbs, etc. The triad of violence makes it all work for you.

HIS INJURY MAY SAVE YOUR LIFE

The goal of violence is injury, which we define as trauma that stops the normal functioning of the body and requires medical attention. These are very important considerations, neither of which says anything about the pain or psychological state of the recipient. Neither of these matters, because different people have different pain thresholds. A torn fingernail drops some into dramatic paroxysms of agony, but for others, a broken limb is bearable. (However, note that while someone with a broken arm may be functional mentally, he won't be able to grab you so easily.)

Injury for the purpose of effective violence is:

1. Objective. Even disinterested third parties would agree that an injury occurred. A badly bleeding, broken leg is obvious from across the street.

2. Detrimental. It alters the normal functioning of his body in a negative way. A broken leg won't allow someone to get up and run quickly after you.

3. Sustained over the course of the encounter. It will require medical attention in order to heal. He can't "walk it off."

I don't mean sprains, bumps, or bruises here. I mean torn ligaments and tendons, broken ribs, a fractured skull, ruptured organs, and other serious damage to tissue. Every injury you inflict must meet all three criteria. If it doesn't, it probably isn't serious enough to cause a spinal reflex or otherwise inhibit his functioning. In other words, uninjured and slightly injured people are free to keep coming at you. And you better bet they will.

Badly injured people, on the other hand, get dropped in their tracks. They are helpless. They cannot stop you from injuring them again. You'll know you've injured him when you elicit a spinal reflex, and while he's incapacitated, you are free to wreck something else in him. For that moment, he literally cannot stop you.

Knowing how to get this done, repeatedly and reliably, grants you incredible power in a violent conflict. But only if you have the will to get it done (intent) and the ability to get it done. It's not enough to want it; you have to have the physical skills that make it a reality. Penetration and rotation are simple to execute (throw your entire body in there and follow all the way through), but it's all going to be for naught if you don't hit a target.

Never expect him to quit. Know that you'll need to render him nonfunctional—clearly unable to get up or even move—and only then will you know it's done. You know twisting his arm won't stop him. You know scratching at his eyes won't, either.

One thing that all survivors have in common (except those rare lucky cases) is that they all believed they could make it out alive. Armed with this belief, their minds used their bodies accordingly, as tools to solve the problem, and they ended up walking out alive. They literally forged the reality they wanted with nothing more than the belief that it could be done, and the mind wielded the tool of the body, fashioning it into a hammer for smashing barriers, a key for unlocking problems, a vehicle for escape. Intent is a very, very powerful tool.

The human brain can figure its way out of almost every jam and then apply the body to the problem. This is why you have to shut an attacker off *now*, regardless of what he's "armed" with, what skills he has, and/or what his physical abilities are.

Now that we've covered all the principles of violence, we're going to explore their application. We're going to combine intent, cause and effect, penetration, and rotation and apply them to anatomical targets in order to injure.

A devastating injury is what you get when you penetrate *through* a man or, if you don't have room, rotate your body to use your body weight to hit and penetrate all the way through the target. These motions are the physical manifestation of applying the principles of violence. They are the methods used for causing injury. Now it's time to put the point on the sword.

The Simplest Form of Injury

"Striking" can be defined as throwing your entire weight against a single target to wreck it. Every method of delivering injury derives its power from striking. Striking is what drives a knife deep into the body and opens the skull with a blow from a stick. It's not pleasant to talk about, but it's how injury gets done.

Ever since caveman days, striking has been the simplest, most intuitive means of causing injury. It's literally as old as fists breaking noses. Despite this, there are entire schools of combat philosophy dedicated to just punching, or kicking, or stick fighting, or knife fighting—heck, even gun fighting. But what if all these seemingly disparate disciplines were linked by common threads? What principles bind a punch, a kick, a stick hitting the head, a stabbing, even a shooting?

PUNCHING VERSUS STRIKING

Imagine you're facing a giant predator and you happen to have a big burlap sack full of rocks. You pull out a rock and throw it at him. It hits him in the shoulder. "Ouch!" he says, advancing toward you. You throw another one at him. Again, "Ouch!" is the only real reaction you get. Now he's pissed and you're running out of rocks.

Eventually, all you have left is an empty bag. You're worn out and can't even lift your arms anymore.

Now imagine that instead of throwing one rock at a time, you'd grabbed the top of the sack with both fists and swung the entire thing at him, hitting him in the head. He'd smack his head on the concrete, down and out cold.

That's the difference between punching and striking.

Instead of looking at each of these things separately, why not start with the desired result—injury—and work backward from there?

Of all the attributes of a strike—speed, snap, structure, weight, accuracy—which one is most important to causing injury? Or is it a combination of them? And if so, in what proportions? Are any of these things useless?

In answering these questions, this chapter will give you the underlying principles that drive all striking.

Let's be very clear: I'm not trying to debunk or contradict any philosophy or technique out there; the goal of this chapter is to teach you how to strike to injure. If you have previous experience or training, this information will enhance your skills and give you new ways to evaluate and apply what you already know. If you have no experience whatsoever, this information will give you the fundamental tools required to use your body as an impact weapon. Either way, my goal right now is to give you the tools to allow you to come out of a violent situation alive.

IT'S *NOT* ABOUT BEING BIG AND STRONG

Whenever conversations about "self-defense" take place, the issue of physicality always comes up. Is strength necessary to defend yourself? And if it's not necessary, is it at least helpful?

The truth is this: While effective striking does require a certain minimum level of physicality (strength, speed, size, etc.), usually a person's physicality is not the Achilles' heel in the whole equation. In other words, surviving a violent encounter requires having sufficient intent, causing the first injury, knowing about targets and how to access them, and yes, possessing a certain amount of physicality.

WEAPONS OF KINETIC ENERGY

While you can deliver large amounts of kinetic energy with your own weight, you can deliver an even more powerful blow using additional weapons, such as sticks, rocks, and guns.

A stick of some kind—including a baseball bat—increases the total KE by adding more mass and acceleration. Because the material your stick is made of is much more dense and rigid than human flesh, when it makes contact with your attacker, his flesh will get the worst of the collision.

A rock is a handy KE reservoir that can be lifted up over your head and used to empty the kinetic energy into his head. And like the stick, rocks are harder than flesh and bone.

A gun is nothing more than a KE reservoir with a delivery system. The powder holds KE in the form of chemical bonds that release the energy upon igniting. The bullet absorbs that energy and takes it to the target to release that energy into the tissues, literally tearing them apart.

This is the ultimate goal of any form of striking: to deliver the largest amount of KE possible into the target to wreck it. And you get that only with a big load of KE.

If you're looking to improve your chances of surviving violence, you should look at all these components and determine which one is your weakest link and then improve upon it. Some women might assume that their smaller size or lesser strength will be this weak link, but I'm here to tell you that it's not. Many children have more than enough physicality to inflict a crippling injury on a big and/or strong man—*if* they have the intent and the knowledge required to do it.

So yes, physicality is indeed needed, but trust me, you likely already have enough. Spend your time becoming intimately familiar with the body's most vulnerable targets and how to strike them.

STRIKING—ALL OF YOU, ALL THE TIME

Imagine the force you would deliver if you hit a man with a bat that weighed as much as you. But that's a physical impossibility, right?

Nope, it's not. Because you *are* the bat! When your body weight is falling, it has far more kinetic energy (KE) in it than your arm can generate alone. Striking is about "falling" on or into him and arresting your fall with some small, hard part of yourself—like your elbow—to deliver all your KE to him.

The most powerful strikes involve using as much of your body weight as you can, all at once. This is what we mean when we say striking is "all of you, all the time."

The most prevalent misconception about striking, particularly among female students who are new to self-defense, is that it's done with your arms and legs. When people think "striking," they usually think of punching and kicking. This leads them to focus on the wrong thing. The goal of striking is to impart the largest possible load of kinetic energy into your target in order to cause injury, and arms and legs aren't able to generate the KE required to cause debilitating injury without fail, every time you strike. An uninjured man can hurt you. If you don't generate enough force, you can't injure and stop him. This likely will make you try any number of other punches and kicks that also won't have sufficient kinetic energy behind them. Targeting will be forgotten and you will end up flailing. There will be no follow-through. He will remain uninjured, and therefore able to hurt you.

And so striking is only and always about applying all the kinetic energy your body can create to your attacker's body to injure him. It's not about punching and kicking, which can't injure him enough to stop him. Striking is about tearing, rupturing, and shattering. Striking is about creating wreckage. To absolutely wreck him, you need the greatest amount of KE you possess.

USE YOUR BODY WEIGHT

Striking without putting your body weight in motion behind it is like throwing bullets at him instead of shooting him. What would you rather do, throw bullets at him or shoot him?

Punching and kicking are akin to slapping him around, while striking creates wreckage. Simply put, every strike must have a result that requires medical attention. Every strike must create an injury. *Anything less than that is pointless.* It's not important how the injury happens, only that it does happen. His ribs don't know if they were broken by a fist, a boot, a stick, a curb, or a car door.

The injury is similar whether he falls and hits his head on a rock or the rock flies through the air and hits him in the head. It doesn't matter which part is in motion and which is stationary; what's important is that he won't be able to come after you.

A big, strong-willed man might be able to withstand more than a few "smacks," but suffering a shattered temporomandibular joint in the jaw and the attendant concussion along with multiple "free" injuries incurred during the knockdown—such as a broken wrist, hyperextended elbow, sprained shoulder, or head trauma—is more than any human can take.

Again: Throw fifty rocks at him, or hit him with the whole sack at once?

THE MOST BASIC STRIKE

In its most basic form, striking is completely artless and without technique. Imagine jumping off your roof and landing on someone. There would be lots of injuries (probably in both of you; you're not immune to physics just because it was your idea), but a lack of technique does not preclude inflicting injury. And it gives us a proof of concept, albeit one that is a bit over the top.

So, in a general sense, the most basic strike is you falling on him.

It uses your body weight, aided by gravity to gain KE, a tool of injury, and targeting to lay it all on him. You fall and use his body as an airbag to arrest your fall. You'll expend all that KE on a single target and make all the injuries his, leaving him feeling as

Practice, Practice, Practice

It's a great idea to practice the two strikes described on page 128. Just understand that the principles and techniques presented in this book are designed for one purpose: to cause serious, debilitating injury or death. Therefore, practicing them can be dangerous. To minimize this inherent danger, please follow these suggestions:

- Work with a partner (ideally a man) who understands and can successfully model the basic concept of the Effect State.

- Work in an environment that's appropriate for safe practice.

- GO SLOW. Targeting is a skill that takes time to develop. You need to practice hitting targets dead-on, with no errors. You need to develop a visceral understanding of where the targets are on someone's body and how to access them from where you are in space. This comes only with slow, steady, and correct though he just got hit by a bus, and you feeling only the gas pedal under your foot. Every strike is based on this concept.

The higher you fall from, the more KE you deliver. If you could carry around a stepladder, clamber up it at the first sign of trouble, and fall on people, you could do a lot of damage to an assailant. (Who knows, maybe someday someone

practice. Fast practice not only is unsafe, but also hinders your targeting. On the street, in a violent situation, you're going to strike him as hard and as fast as you can. But until you possess the underlying skill of targeting, you might miss and be ineffective. Try to work at the speed of tai chi practice, or, to put it another way, go slower than feels comfortable.

■ When we work on technique in my classes, I do not allow the participants to talk to each other. This type of work is psychologically uncomfortable, and you'll likely be self-conscious and nervous, at least at first. You'll try to relieve your discomfort by talking because your subconscious mind is trying to turn an asocial scenario into a social one. In real asocial violence, talking may get you killed. If you abide by this rule in your practice, you'll get a much better result should you ever need to use it on the street.

will market a self-defense stepladder, but not now—and not me.)

To keep things simple, let's assume that the highest point you can fall from is your height in a standing position. This is the position you're most likely to find yourself in while out and about. And it's loaded with KE.

An ideal strike, then, is to fall on a person who is lying on the ground, landing on your knees and driving them into your target, crushing it. It doesn't matter if he's facedown or faceup; the human body is target-rich either way. If he's faceup, you can crush his testicles; if he's facedown, you could drop onto the spine in his lower back.

It's nearly artless, being barely more difficult than simply falling on him, with the only additions being tools (the elbow or knees) and the choice of a specific target. But as you can see, these minor additions begin to make a big difference: They convert raw, unbridled KE into predictable, reproducible trauma.

So the most basic strike consists of kinetic energy, the use of an appropriate tool, and a target. If we remove any one element or try to use only one of them, the results become haphazard, inefficient, and uncertain.

THE TWO SIMPLEST, MOST EFFECTIVE STRIKES

Right now, as you're reading this, I'd like you to get up and practice the two strikes I'm about to teach you. If you're alone, that's fine, just execute these strikes against an imaginary adversary for now (a pillow or a stuffed chair works well). Later, you can practice with a partner (please read the sidebar on page 126 about how to practice first!).

Imagine that a large man is standing right in front of you—and that's all. Don't worry about what he might be doing or anything else; you're simply going to injure him.

Your target is the front of his neck, which is super delicate and easy to access. The neck is a worthwhile target from any angle (back, front, or sides), and it can be reached if the man is standing, sitting, or lying (for example, if he's lying facedown or faceup, you can drop your knee onto his neck with devastating result).

The striking surface we'll use is your forearm (technically your ulna, which is the bone on the pinkie side of your forearm), about two to three inches above your wrist. You might wonder why I'm not saying to use your fist. The reason is that the hand comprises twenty-seven bones, making it a relatively fragile striking device. Since your ulna is always ready to go, use that instead.

Your ulna will be the pointy, super-hard "hood ornament" on your "truck," which, of course, is your body. Now, look at the attacker's neck and raise your dominant arm, which should be sharply bent, forearm parallel to the floor, palm facing downward. Step in toward your target and strike toward the clavicle or base of the neck so you can continue pushing upward instead of aiming too high and missing completely. It doesn't matter which leg you step in with; the important thing is to just step in.

If you find you're reaching for the target, you're not penetrating! Step *into* the man so that by the time you complete the strike, you're standing where he used to be. Run over him with the truck (your body), hitting him with the hood ornament (your forearm). Don't reach; use your entire body to move forward. Raise your arm in front of your body, step *in*, and run him down, plowing your ulna into his throat with all the force you can muster.

If you've done this successfully, he's *reacting* to your strike (as discussed in Chapter Seven) and is leaning back, grasping his throat in agony. In this reflexive posture, his groin is exposed and vulnerable to attack. You're going to exploit this reflexive reaction by piling on the next injury, which will be caused by a knee to the groin.

Just like the neck, the groin can be struck from many angles (front, behind, above, etc.) and with many tools (your hand, foot, knee, or elbow, or a club, etc.). In this example, you'll be driving your knee into his testicles as you're standing facing each other.

Remember, you're going to use the entire mass of your body; you're not simply reaching out and touching his groin with your knee. Think of taking your knee to his groin as an exaggerated step: As you step forward, his groin gets in the way of your knee. The strike will actually displace him, knocking him away from you, and you'll now be standing where he *used* to be.

Although I've shown you only two different strikes in this chapter, it's not difficult to expand your arsenal by using your imagination and creativity. What other vulnerable targets can you injure with your hands, elbows, knees, or feet, or even with a tool such as a briefcase or a rock?

For example, is your attacker's foot vulnerable to injury? You bet. How might you most easily strike it? By stomping down on it with your entire weight? Of course.

Are your attacker's eyes a vulnerable target? Absolutely. How can you injure them? By ramming your fingers (or a pen, or almost anything) into them as hard as you can.

Practice striking targets using the tips in the sidebar on page 126. Remember: When it comes to violence, practice may never make perfect, but it will absolutely give you an advantage for surviving the most unthinkable situations.

CHAPTER NINE

FEARLESS FOREVER

ear is a biological reality. We are hardwired for fight or flight—remember, we're the descendants of the ones who didn't stop to think when the lion was bearing down on them. We're the kin of the ones who literally "went ape" and either raised a rooster tail of dust toward the horizon or picked up a stick and got busy. But just because fear is a biological fact doesn't mean that we have to give in to it—we don't have to feed the fear, allow it to grow fat on the shadows of our nightmares. We can recognize (and be grateful for) the lifesaving benefits of biological fear without letting it consume us with emotional panic.

We do this by killing the unknown.

Most people have no idea what goes on in a violent encounter: We assume it is terrifying, painful, chaotic, or worse. It is a Great Unknown, something we think happens only to other people, not to us. Violence is something we try not to think about. But what if you replace that scary unknown with knowledge and understanding? You will take away the power of the unknown and starve it until it is a manageable size. Then, the fear of violence and the unthinking, blind panic that it induces will become simple biological fear. "Flight" means you get the hell out of there. "Fight" means you stomp and tear and wreak horror upon the other guy.

There are two ways to make sure you're familiar with the terrain shown on the violence map and changing "Oh my god!" to "Slam boot to groin." The first (and most important) is practice; the other is simple visualization. Both of these serve the same function: They help you look at and understand what is currently unfamiliar, frightening territory.

Each practice session is an expedition into that Great Unknown to lay bare its secrets, to pretend you are facing down a creepy dude on a dark street. Every time you visualize or practice, you're answering the question "What the hell happens now?" Move by move, you answer that question, completely and with certitude: I crush his groin, I tear out his eye, I break his neck. I walk away. That's what happens. Mystery solved.

BE YOUR OWN HERO

As you continue to practice and train, you may experience what I call the "zombie dream": You've been attacked and you're tearing into the guy, breaking his leg, stomping his throat—but he keeps getting back up. So you do it again. And still he rises and comes at you. No one is coming to save you. You have to do it by yourself.

We've all seen people that gave us pause, for one reason or another—he wasn't just big, he was enormous, he had a swastika tattooed on his face, and he looked like he was at the end of his rope; or he just seemed scary, you didn't quite know why. These frightening monsters might have kept you up at night, but now you can fight back in your dreams.

You know he's human. He bleeds. And if he bleeds, you can injure him so that he can't injure you. You have to remind yourself of this fact and give yourself permission to become violent if it's necessary to save your own life. Practice visualizing yourself in a situation like that in the zombie dream, when you're protecting yourself, inflicting one injury after another, putting him down and then escaping, alive. Imagine it in slo-mo, watching yourself execute each strike, or speed it up, running through sequences of moves to fix them in your mind. This is how you acknowledge two important truths: No one is immune from violence, and you know how to use violence if you have to. There is no such thing as a one-eyed ogre; he is just a man who won't be able to hurt you because you won't let him. You are your own hero.

When violence is thoroughly mapped out and you are presented with option after option in real time, you know what to expect. There is no more Great Unknown to swallow you up in a blind panic. As we replace the unknown with knowledge, we isolate fear down to its biological roots and inhibit its ability to grow unchecked in your mind. Instead of giving in to it, feeding it, helping it, you'll use it for what it's for— putting your boot in the other guy's groin. And after that, the rest is academic.

AN OUNCE OF PREVENTION

Remember way back at the beginning of this book, when we discussed how having a better knowledge of violence tells you when *not* to use it? The goal of really understanding violence is to, hopefully, keep you from ever having to use it. As I've stressed again and again, you should never use violence unless you're in a life-or-death situation. That still holds true. And you can take steps to keep yourself out of life-or-death situations in the first place.

Many of us have the impression that violent situations could never happen to us. We hear about violence all the time in the news, but unless it's right next door—unless it directly affects us, or someone we love—we continue to believe that we're sheltered and somehow protected from criminal violence.

While it's true that most of us are fortunate enough not to live in a war zone or a military police state, we have to acknowledge that criminal sociopaths exist everywhere, and they're ready and willing to use serious force to get whatever it is they want.

With that in mind, here are a few simple steps you can take to protect yourself on a daily basis.

- ✧ Always immediately lock your doors once you're inside your home or your car.
- ✧ Be careful when handling money, especially at ATMs. Know who's behind you, and don't flash your cash around; quickly put it in your bag or pocket and walk away.

- Avoid dark, isolated spaces, bars known for trouble, and anywhere else you get an uneasy feeling.
- Don't leave spare keys under doormats or in other obvious places.
- Remain vigilant: Keep your eyes open for strange people and situations and, whenever possible, avoid them.

If you do find yourself in an uncomfortable situation, just walk away. Don't allow someone who is clearly unstable to draw you into a violent encounter. You may feel like you're hurting your pride by not getting in that last word, but you've really won by preventing a situation that might lead to serious harm.

Learning how to use violence properly is about protecting yourself in a dangerous situation—it doesn't replace your common sense. If you walk around with blinders on, you're much more likely to encounter violence, even if you're in what you think is a perfectly safe environment. Self-awareness is the best first step in avoiding the unthinkable.

STUPID IS AS STUPID DOES

If a convicted murderer escapes from prison and kills someone, no one is much surprised. If the murderer is killed by his intended victim, it's a "job well done." But if two innocent people get into a situation where no one means to kill anyone and someone ends up dead, well, then it's cartoon exclamation points all around. Everyone, including the newly minted killer, is surprised. Cries of "How could this have happened?" and "But I didn't want to kill him!" ring out. In the end, it's usually labeled an unfortunate accident or self-defense.

We don't expect someone to die in a bar fight. And yet death is one of the possible outcomes.

My aversion to violence runs so strong that it makes me something of a contradiction to my friends—I will do whatever I can to avoid physical, antisocial confrontations and yet wouldn't hesitate to stomp someone into the morgue in the asocial realm. I'm like Gandhi with a nuclear weapon.

If someone tries to attack you, you're now prepared—knowledgeable, practiced, resolute. But don't forget to sharpen those skills, and think about how you want to act in those situations. Will you join in and play along? Throw fuel on the fire? Push until he either backs down or goes for you? Or will you go completely sideways on him by defusing the situation, seeking to reduce his fear and channel his anger elsewhere?

Know what your triggers are and put lots of padding between them and the outside world. Work to recognize when you're being pushed into a corner. And remember that simply walking away could save your life, too.

Remember: Be prepared. Chances are you'll go your entire life without anyone trying to kill you. I wouldn't make the same bet about some jerk trying to cop a feel, though.

A FINAL WORD

My definition of fighting is very different from what people might think it is: I view fighting as inflicting trauma on the human body by using specific methods, with the goal being the destruction of the other guy. In the rare instances when I've decided to speak about fighting in a social situation, I usually regret doing so. I quickly see that most people are uncomfortable with my calm descriptions of the effective use of violence.

Hopefully, you now understand my perspective, and know that my definition of violence is not the same as the definition presented in movies or video games. I teach people how to methodically deliver systematic strikes to vulnerable parts of the human body in order to end a conflict. The better trained you are to understand real violence, the more relaxed you become emotionally—and the more you get to enjoy your life rather than fearing the unknown.

You've taken the initiative to learn about violence and how to use it when necessary. You're now not only better prepared to handle any dangerous situation that might come up, but also free from experiencing unnecessary fear of violence in your day-to-day life. Now, that's empowering.

Whether it's a drunken stranger demanding that you pay for an accidentally spilled drink or an overly friendly businessman leaning in a little too close, learn to recognize the warning signs of violence and don't let them control you. It's true that these situations can become violent—but most of the time, they don't. Learn to walk away. Avoid the unthinkable. You have the responsibility to choose *not* to do violence unless no choice remains. However, if the unthinkable happens, you now also know how to cause serious injury and even death. This knowledge is very powerful, and with continued practice it will stay with you for the rest of your life.

By using the tools in this book, you will be able to recognize and distinguish between antisocial aggression and asocial violence, respond with deadly precision to a real violent attack, and control any situation so you survive it. You are the one in charge. My aim in teaching you how to use violence is to allow you to have control of your own life. Once it's yours, live it well.

ACKNOWLEDGMENTS

Dynamic is a description that does not do my wife, Sasha, justice; she provides an incredible support system for me and puts up with my crazy work schedule, world travel, and numerous additional projects I've taken on (like writing this book). She is a wife, mother, police sergeant, accomplished martial artist, and world-class yoga instructor. Her job brings her face-to-face with asocial violence on a regular basis, and she prefers to work in the most crime-challenged parts of our city. Yet despite seeing the worst humanity has to offer, she lives a balanced life, and if you met her, you would never know the world she deals with in her work. As I write this, she is pregnant with twin girls, and I can think of no better role model for those young women. My thanks to her for providing me with a true avatar of what a woman is capable of when it comes to self-protection.

To my sons, Conner and Brock, you guys inspire me every day to be a better person, instructor, and father.

I'd also like to thank the many women I've trained over the years in self-protection (too numerous to mention) and the many contributions they have made to this book. Many have truly survived the unthinkable and were passionate about ensuring that the information in this book gives women the tools necessary to navigate the world of asocial violence and avoid the world of antisocial behavior.

Thanks to master Target Focus Training instructor Chris Ranck-Buhr for all his insights and assistance whenever I hit a roadblock with this material. I am fortunate to have Chris as a keystone to Target Focus Training. His knowledge of the material and his formidable physical mastery of the system are unparalleled, yet he treats every new student as his first chance to share this information. He is the most egoless true master I've ever come across in my many years of being in this crazy business. In a self-defense world rife with egomaniacs and charlatans (without a fraction of his ability), he is truly that piece of gold in the sea of rubble that is the self-defense industry.

Thanks to my business partner, Ralph Charlton, for all his support and keeping the business of TFT running smoothly as I travel and train worldwide. Ralph is my favorite person to brainstorm with, and he provided many edits and suggestions that made this book much better.

Thanks to my friend Charles Staley, who agreed to help compile and edit this huge manuscript and edit it down to the book you have in your hands. Charles is an incredible writer and world-class coach in the fitness world, and it was great to rely on his expertise as an author of numerous books and publications.

I'd like to give my thanks on so many levels to Tony Robbins. He sought me out for his own self-protection training (as well as for his family and friends), then, after the experience, became a passionate advocate for Target Focus Training. He had me present to his clients worldwide and opened more doors for me than he will ever know. He pushed me to write the book you have in your hands. I've met many VIPs and celebrities in my twenty-plus years of doing this work, and few walk the walk of their talk. Tony is the real deal!

I'd like to thank Steven Pressfield, author of so many great books (*Gates of Fire* and *War on Art,* to name two), for planting the seed of writing a book in me more than nine years ago when he graciously took me to dinner in Malibu after spending the afternoon with me at his home. He asked me many questions and then told me I had a few books in me whether I realized it or not. That stuck with me and encouraged me on my path.

To Ursula Cary, Jess Fromm, Chris Krogermeier, Nancy Bailey, Amy King, Chris Gaugler, Nancy Elgin, Beth Bazar, and the rest of the team at Rodale Books: Thanks for taking a chance on me and giving me the support necessary to get this information out to women everywhere.

My sincere thanks to Jan Miller; Shannon Marven; my agent, Lacy Lynch; and the whole support team at Dupree/Miller. You all really made it easy for me as I navigated the publishing world for the first time. The personal stories you shared with me about women and violence really showed me your passion for helping me get this book to a female audience.

Index

Boldface page references indicate illustrations.
Underscored references indicate boxed text.

About the Author

Tim Larkin is a self-protection expert and the creator of the Target Focus Training (TFT) system, his own method of teaching self-defense, modeled after his experience training US Navy SEALs, Army Special Forces, and other law enforcement agents all over the world. For 20 years, he has taught his clients—celebrities, children, parents, athletes, and corporate execs alike—how to think like a predator and how to retaliate in a targeted way for maximum impact with only minimal physical strength required.

A sought-after public speaker, Larkin has spoken to CEOs, government officials, and business leaders in more than 40 countries on how to use these same principles of surviving life-or-death violence in the less life-threatening environment of business. He's been featured in *Forbes*, *Muscle & Fitness*, *Black Belt* magazine, *London Financial Times*, and on msnbc.com, BBC.com, and other outlets, and he was named *Black Belt* magazine's 2011 Self-Defense Instructor of the Year. He is the coauthor of *How to Survive the Most Critical 5 Seconds of Your Life*.

For more information, visit www.survivetheunthinkable.com or targetfocustraining.com.